Herbert Scherer

IF YOU DOUBT in God

Against all odds, God brought a young soldier back alive
from the Siberian death camps

(Based on his true life's story)

Note for Librarians: a cataloguing record for this book that includes Dewey Decimal Classification and US Library of Congress numbers is available from the Library and Archives of Canada. The complete cataloguing record can be obtained from their online database at:
www.collectionscanada.ca/amicus/index-e.html
ISBN 1-4120-4620-3
Printed in Victoria, BC, Canada

TRAFFORD

Offices in Canada, USA, Ireland, UK and Spain
This book was published *on-demand* in cooperation with Trafford Publishing. On-demand publishing is a unique process and service of making a book available for retail sale to the public taking advantage of on-demand manufacturing and Internet marketing. On-demand publishing includes promotions, retail sales, manufacturing, order fulfilment, accounting and collecting royalties on behalf of the author.
Book sales for North America and international:
Trafford Publishing, 6E–2333 Government St.,
Victoria, BC v8t 4p4 CANADA
phone 250 383 6864 (toll-free 1 888 232 4444)
fax 250 383 6804; email to orders@trafford.com
Book sales in Europe:
Trafford Publishing (uk) Ltd., Enterprise House, Wistaston Road Business Centre,
Wistaston Road, Crewe, Cheshire cw2 7rp UNITED KINGDOM
phone 01270 251 396 (local rate 0845 230 9601)
facsimile 01270 254 983; orders.uk@trafford.com
Order online at:
www.trafford.com/robots/04-2428.html

10 9 8 7 6 5 4 3 2

Preface

1928 Recognition of a Higher Power.
It was challenging to experience the horrors of the battlefield, the deprivations of war, the inhumanities dealt on
a daily basis, and connect them to the undeniable graces
that came to my aid throughout this six year period. My
story is what I experienced, and the fact that I attribute my
survival to a higher power. I drew upon that higher power
to sustain me when there was really no hope; no rescue
possible.

Where does such power come from? When and how
did it manifest itself?

I look back to the year 1928, when I was three and a
half years old. My little sister, Gertrude, was only six and a
half, and had just begun to attend school. For the first time
in my short lifetime, I felt lonely. My mother reassured
me that Gertrude would come home by noon to play with
me. I waited. Finally, she arrived at eleven o'clock. She
walked in importantly. Like a star. I was curious. I wanted
to know exactly what she had learned at school, whether it
was mathmatics, or the art of writing. But to my surprise,
she replied emphatically, "None of that!"

She explained to me that they learned about Jesus all
morning. Gertrude was attending a Catholic convent and

being taught by English nuns. It all sounded so interesting. I begged her to tell me everything she could about this Jesus.

My mother sat a little away from the table, listening attentively. I stood on her left side with my elbows on her leg; Gertrude was on the other side, telling us her story. Sometimes Mama corrected her, or added something.

After Gertrude finished her story, I was silent because what I heard shocked me. I was also sad and angry. I wanted to do something about what I heard, but I did not know what I could do.

Young as I was, I saw clearly how cruel and unjust this world could be. How was it possible that people could murder Jesus, who was born so humbly and who was the Son of God!?

He, who healed so many of the sick in his lifetime had been condemned to such a death as the crucifixion. It made no sense to me.

It was at this point that I decided to go visit Jesus to bring him comfort and to tell him how much I loved Him. But that would have to wait. Dusk came. I went to bed. Waiting for sleep, I had the feeling that peace, security and warmth could only be found in my parents' home. Outside our front door was the raw, insensitive world, waiting to hurt me. Eventually sleep came over me, as it comes so readily to a child.

After breakfast the next morning I went out to play with the other children. It was just after Easter, and mild outside. But I really did not feel like playing. Instead I walked about a kilometer to our church. A child was safe walking alone in those years.

The church appeared immense to me. It was a two-tower structure made of natural beige sandstone blocks, fitted perfectly into place. As I approached, I noticed that one of the huge, solid oak doors had been left ajar. I could never have opened it by myself. Even the handle was too high for me to reach. I entered the sanctuary. There was not a soul inside. I was happy that I could be alone here.

I walked slowly toward the front, where I chose to sit on the second bench. There was an enormous crucifix hanging on the wall behind the altar. As I looked at it, my sadness was overpowering. Then I smiled with relief as I remembered my sister's story that on Easter Jesus came out of his grave and returned to his Heavenly Father. I knew then that He could hear me and that He knew all about me.

I felt that I was in His presence; that He was giving me time to settle down and treasure the moment.

I did not say a word for a long time. I felt that his eyes were on me. But He, also, was silent.

After awhile I told Him that I came because I loved Him, and that I was sad about His sufferings. I wanted to stay, hoping that He could find a little consolation and joy in my presence. Then I thought that perhaps I should have brought Him some kind of gift. But what, after all, could a little child bring? Besides, this was the time of the great depression, and we had so little to live on. I addressed him once more, "Jesus, I have nothing to give You but my love and my friendship."

There was no answer, but I felt a reassurance that He was now my friend.

Since then, I went back often, and always found that same, profound peace and gentle love waiting for me. Mark: 10,15: "Truly I say unto you, whoever does not receive the Kingdom of God like a child, will by no means enter into it."

*****

A child has many doors opened by chance, and by a willingness to receive with an open mind.

One night, when I was four years old, I was transported by means of an unexpectedly meaningful dream to a place too beautiful to describe.

My first sensation was mildness, followed by a wonderful, sweet fragrance. I was in a strange place. The trees all had coloured leaves. Strangely, the sky was not blue, nor did the sun shine down upon me, but a warm light shone from a honey-colored sky. Several beings dressed in pure white robes walked slowly but steadily toward me, their arms invitingly extended They had different hair styles and skin colors. They called to me by name, saying they were expecting me.

How could this be?

Taking me by the hand they brought me to a place where we could all sit in a circle. Their faces radiated love, calm and goodness. Physically, they appeared to be young women about twenty years of age, and their skin, hair and eyes appeared to be perfect and healthy. I felt absolutely safe and secure. Night did not fall and I was never tired.

For a moment I believed that I had died and gone to heaven. In all my joy, I forgot the real world. But the real world had not forgotten me. As quickly as the dream began, it ended.

Upon awakening I wondered what had just happened to me. I knew I was back in my room, and I knew I was alive. Within three short hours the sun would rise again, and my daily chores would resume. Reluctant to let go of the beautiful dream, I was forced to accept the reality. I cried, but not loudly enough to wake my parents sleeping in the adjacent bedroom.

What a strange dream. Yet, it was so powerful. So real!

This experience came back to me over and over again until I reached the age of nineteen. Then it never returned.

But what could be the significance of such a dream?

Matthew 11:25: At that time, Jesus said in response: "I publicly praise you Father, Lord of Heaven and earth because you have hidden these things from the wise and the intellectual, yet have revealed them to babes."

*****

1929

At age five my greatest fear was that some day, someone would come and prove to me that God did not exist. Could it be possible that God was only a legend, like Santa Clause?

If that should be, the world would certainly become

a cold star for me. It would no longer offer security or love. Yes, if God did not exist I believed that mankind was doomed. Only He could bring a measure of dignity and justice to the world.

*****

Acknowledgement

I wish to take this opportunity to thank God for all that He has done for me throughout my life. He has helped me to accomplish my mission on earth through His love, His power, and His grace. Without Him, I could never have survived. He had His plan for me. The song below depicts how I feel. It may also reflect how you feel.

Amazing Grace

1. Amazing grace how sweet the sound
   That saved a wretch like me!
   I once was lost, but now I am found,
   Was blind, but now I see.

2. 'Twas grace that taught my heart to fear,
   And grace my fears relieved;
   How precious did that grace appear
   The hour I first believed!

3. The Lord has promised good to me,
   His word my hope secures;

He will my shield and portion be
As long as life endures.

4. Through many dangers toils and snares.
   I have already come;
   'Tis grace has brought me safe thus far,
   And grace will lead me home.

5. When we've been there ten thousand years,
   Bright shining as the sun,
   We've no less days to sing God's praise
   Than when we'd first begun.

John Newton, 1725-1807

Dedication

This book is dedicated to God, who, in His love, has worked many miracles to keep me alive, even though I did not expect it. Especially where survival seemed no longer possible. Also, I dedicate this work to my grandfather, who was always there in my life, supporting me, and waiting for me to come back from the torturous Siberian death camps. Unfortunately, he died three months before I returned home.

My Special Prayer

Please Lord, give me the strength to continue on the path of my life.

Let me walk humbly in your light. I praise you, my Lord, and I declare your love and righteousness without fear.

Amen

Herbert Scherer

Table of Contents

Chapter One
Germany

1933

I was only nine years old when Adolph Hitler came to power in 1933. But children grow up quickly in hard times, and I was old enough to realize what he stood for in Germany: "Might is Right."

I also realized, even with my child's vision, that politics was a dirty and dangerous game. Political envy and conflict arose from the fact that the Western nations could not provide employment for its own working classes, while Germany enjoyed full employment.

1939

In September, France and England declared war on Germany following Hitler's aggression against Poland and Czechoslovakia. This did not displease Hitler because it meant that with several nations embroiled in the terrible devastation that war always brings, his military would create its own industry. After all, his armies would need ammunition, uniforms, food, transportation, and so on.

Factories started hiring. Germany's economic situation improved. Money flowed again. Unfortunately, so did the blood of countless millions of its citizens.

1942

In the spring I was drafted into the German army. Standing naked in front of ten officers, I was asked under which command of the armed forces I wanted to serve.

Draftees had a choice because we were the youngest. I was the only man that day, among the three hundred, who chose to enter the infantry, to serve on the Eastern Front.

Thinking, perhaps, that I had not clearly understood the consequences of such a choice, one of the commanding officers asked me if I knew what I was doing. I reassured him that this was where I felt that I could do my part in order to keep Stalin and Communism out of Europe and, out of Germany.

Time is of the essence in war. We had to be prepared quickly. Three months of extremely tough basic training followed. In fact, so rigid and demanding was this training that some even committed suicide. Having a lot of energy and stamina, I survived.

The battalion commander enlisted me in a school for officers, but my heart was not in it. I knew that the real heroes were those on the battlefield.

August, 1943

In the last days of August we said our good-byes to our loved ones and headed directly for the Russian front line by train. In comfortless cattle cars, we rolled and wormed our way all day toward the east, crossing a ravaged Germany, then into Poland.

By the second morning we were well into western

Russia. The villages we passed through displayed a pitiful air of poverty.

I found myself liking the native Russian people more and more as we rode along. Theirs was a degree of unpretentiousness that I had never seen before. Their houses were made of logs. There did not seem to be running water, or electricity. There were not even any roads or visible means of transportation. Not bicycles, cars or trucks.

I don't know how these impoverished Russian citizens survived because there did not seem to be even oil, or wood for their cooking, or to keep them warm.

Due to stoney soil and endless forests the land was largely uncultivated. Impoverished crops led the people an impoverished existence.

Our train wound its way southward, stopping briefly, then changing directions northward to arrive, finally, at our destination.

Here, we were unloaded at Mogilev.

We were a group of one hundred men. Our sergeant received our marching orders. We marched for several days without incident. Food was scarce so every second day we stopped to try to find some nourishment. We were hungry all the time.

Here the land was different than in Germany. It was flat. There were scattered fields here and there, guarded by pine forests. Finally we came upon a few villages.

Poorly dressed women carried water to their houses from a common village well. A few starved horses pulled loads too heavy for their weakened physical condition.

The Russian Bolsheviks had reduced the area to abject poverty, returning it to the stone age.

By next evening we arrived at another small village on the shores of the Djepper River. Here we were invited to carry hay into one of the houses to make our beds, and gratefully settled down for a welcome sleep.

The owner of this dwelling was a fairly old man with a long white beard. He was accompanied by his wife and daughter, and her infant.

The only diversion available was conversation. So during the evening in spite of the language barrier, we managed to talk together. It pleased us to make the woman of the house proud by our admiring comments about her daughter's baby. However, duty would soon call us back to war, and so we bedded down to sleep.

I awoke at five o'clock in the morning. Others were awake also. I heard them whispering. Glancing around the room I saw the devout old man with his family gathered facing the altar in the far corner. Apparently, as soon as the Bolsheviks left a village, the Russian families remaining would each build a small altar in a corner of their one-room houses.

The old man prayed earnestly, tears trickling down his cheeks and onto his beard. Imagine, I came all this way to witness a man pray like that. I would never forget his tears of faith.

The next day the Sergeant gathered us into our marching columns and told us, "Today, we march for our own good," whatever that meant. After a very long time, marching without rest, I asked the Sergeant our destination. "Leave that to the horses," he said. "They have bigger heads."

As we marched toward the east, thousands of Russian refugee families moved in long columns toward the west, fleeing from the advancing Russian Red Army.

They walked, young and old, behind little horse-drawn wagons. The older grandmothers drove little horse wagons, Holding the reins loosely in their hands they were seated, half asleep, on bags of grain, letting their heads bob up and down and to and fro. They looked downward, lost in thought and hopelessness. Not one of them said a word.

Nothing in my life saddened me more than the sight of this endless gray line of human misery extending to the horizon. Not one of these unfortunates knew where they would lay their heads for the night. Nor did they know what the next day would bring.

When they left their villages, they lost everything they had ever worked for. Their homeland, the land of their youth, their dreams destroyed by the Bolshevik Regime. They had not chosen to become refugees in their own land, but that was their unfortunate situation. Most of them ended up in Poland or Germany. The young ones buried their parents there, got married, and stayed, or moved on to the U.S.A. or Canada.

It was cold when we arrived at our destination in September. Winter was not far. We paused on the edge of a pine forest. Here we met a Corporal who explained the situation. Our front line of defense was just one kilometer ahead. The sun was on the peak of the horizon now, just starting to set.

Chapter Two
The Front Line

When we arrived at the trenches, our future group leader greeted us. He was a little man, with fear in his eyes.

Our trench snaked its way along the high shore of the Sozc River. In back of us stood a row of eight houses with barns. There was a deep decline in front of the trench, and a barbed wire barrier along the edge of the water. The river was about twenty meters wide and several meters deep. Beyond that stretched a swamp, which extended for at least two kilometers, right to the edge of a pine forest, which was the Russian position.

Sometimes we could go for days without hearing one shot. It must have been the best stretch of front line that could be found on the Eastern Front. I felt that, with a commanding view of the river below, and the entire swamp between us, the Russians would never attack.

With winter coming, however, it didn't take long to realize that the swamp and the river would freeze, providing a wide path for our enemy to use to cross over.

Next morning we decided to build a bunker that could withstand an artillery attack. So we dug an immense hole about the size of a bathhouse that we had seen nearby and set to work. We constructed this bunker out of dismantled pine logs from a cabin. We had numbered all the logs, then built it up again in the excavation. We even installed a door and two bunk beds, which we piled high with straw for a soft mattress. The bunker would protect us from being wiped out by the Russian artillery fire, and the comfort was enough to give us all a chance to sleep. It was "home" for ten men. Since there were six men on guard duty day and night, it afforded us more than enough room to sleep.

The platoon leader, a Sergeant from Saxonia, came to me while I was on watch. We had a good conversation about home, which made the time pass a little faster. A two-hour watch is an eternity when a soldier is alone. Much to my surprise, the sergeant told me that in the morning I was to take my gear and move it to the platoon commander's bunker. He wanted me to be his personal messenger but, because nothing was happening, I was more a bodyguard than anything else. I was free to do what I wanted most of the day.

One of my daytime activities included peeling and boiling the red potatoes that we found in a nearby hay barn.

In the villagers' abandoned dwellings we found a small barrel of honey and several barrels of salted cucumbers, pickled with dill and garlic.

With all of that, we could keep our bodies going. Our army food was monotonous, and too heavy. Like bean soup dense enough to be eaten with a fork.

Looking at that small village, I could see that the people, if left alone and free, could have lived a simple, healthy life. But there was certainly no luxury. They made their own cloth from which to make their clothing; between the houses, up to the edge of the forest, they had nice fields to cultivate. The forest provided all the wood they needed to build their homes, and to use as fire wood to heat them. I truly believe that life makes a lot of sense if we keep it simple and remember God.

By appreciating their humble life style, I understood and loved the people of this land, who were happy with less. All they wanted was to live, work hard, and so fulfill their lives.

Instead, Moscow intervened, letting them know just who had absolute power over life and death in this tortured land. Thus, they had to abandon the contentment of the simple life that was all they had ever known and wanted, and walk away from this wonderful little jewel of land nestled in the quiet countryside. What a social tragedy! But, of course, this is war.

*****

The autumn days had turned mild, and the trees were glorious in their bright colors. Wild geese landed on the river. It was beautiful to watch, but they were also a source of food for our survival. As I watched them land on the river, I noticed some big fish feeding lazily near the surface of the water. My mouth began to water and hunger pains again cramped my hollow stomach. Without hesitation I pulled out the pin from one of my grenades and threw it near the center of the river. It sank and then exploded deep down. The water boiled and bubbled from the explosion. In delight I saw six big muskies floating to the surface.

Using a nearby dug-out tree trunk, I paddled out to retrieve them.

My hunger, and that of my company and the company commander, reaped the succulent harvest. At noon the next day, which was a Sunday, the Sergeant-Major invited the Sergeant and myself to his bunker for a feast of fish steaks, red potatoes with salted cucumber and garlic. While the afternoon sun shone through a little window on the west side of the bunker, we relaxed with coffee, and chatted contentedly about "back home." It really was a splendid afternoon, and the best time I had on the Sozc River, or anywhere else on the front line. One of the good memories to treasure.

September 1943

One night, near the end of September, a Russian double agent approached the bank on the other side of the river. He told us his name, and said that he wanted to come over to our side. We told him that he would have to wait until morning. At daybreak he was picked up and brought to the commander for questioning.

At this point, our Captain went on leave and was replaced by a young Lieutenant who wanted to play Napoleon. A few nights later we heard another Russian crying out that he, too, wanted to be taken across the river. We warned the young Lieutenant not to go on the river during the night, but he insisted on going with two Corporals to pick up the Russian. They ventured out into the river on a raft. When they came to the center, the Russians opened fire with automatic weapons, killing all three.

Another of our young officers became enraged by this and wanted to pursue these Russian snipers and take them prisoner to get more information. What information did he need? After all, we were here in the trenches to defend our position on the front line from a mass attack and nothing else. Still, the officer ordered my Sergeant to do the patrol.

We could see by the clear light of the moon that the swamp had not yet frozen. The river, however, had broken sheets of ice, moving fast. We three were to cross this river on a raft by means of a steel cable stretched from shore to shore. We had to hang onto this cable and pull our way across, always fighting against the rush of the strong current and hampered by the broken ice.

Arriving on the other shore, I did not climb up the bank because I had to go back to get the Sergeant and the second messenger, a pleasant young man whose name was Epstein.

By now the weather had changed. The moonlight was blocked out by clouds and it was very dark. Even with my good night vision, I could see nothing. About the center of the river, the Sergeant's voice rang out urgently just beside me: "Let the cable go, let the cable go!" In the same instant, we collided. The Sergeant and Epstein were thrown into the water. Epstein drowned; the Sergeant swam to the German side, and I floated uncontrollably in the grasp of the current toward the Russian Line.

I paddled with my hands and feet to gain control of my direction, but my efforts were in vain. I could not turn the raft. I abandoned the raft and swam to the nearest shore which, unfortunately, happened to be the side of the Russian controlled territory.

I had to swim between the broken ice floes and by the time I arrived on the shore I was too cold to crawl onto the land. Here two German soldiers saw me and pulled me to my feet.

My clothes had frozen stiff on me. Fearful as we were of getting caught by some Russian patrol, we had to call to our side for help. A few of our German comrades heard us. They quickly nailed two dugouts together and came to our rescue. Since my clothes were frozen rigid, I had to stand in the dugout.

Once on our shore, someone brought me to the company bunker where a soldier undertook to give me a good rubdown to restore my circulation, while another thoughtfully hung up my frozen clothes near the wood stove to dry.

Someone else prepared a hot drink made of black tea, honey and brandy. They called this drink "The Bear Catcher." Within minutes my body was glowing and alive again. My Sergeant, in the bed next to mine, received a similar treatment, and was soon in excellent spirits.

Once more I realized how very lucky I had been. I had escaped death in the icy waters. It would have been easy for the Russian soldiers to send up a signal light to spot us. They could easily have killed us in a hail of bullets. I was soon back on duty. My new role in the trenches was to coordinate the four machine gun posts during the night shift. The posts were a hundred meters apart, and I was to walk this critical three hundred-meter trench in the dark of night. Fortunately I had excellent night vision and acute hearing. I was like a hunting dog, stopping every so often to catch the slightest sound. Then again, I suppose that you never really hear the shot that kills you.

Dec. 1, 1943

While making my rounds I arrived safely at the last post on the far left extremity of our platoon. Three young gunners, about my age, from Luxembourg (between France and Germany), asked for the password, which I gave them. One of them then beckoned me and asked in a whisper if we would ever get home again. The night was bitterly cold, and so dark that we could scarcely see each other's faces. As I turned to respond, suddenly I had an uncanny vision. Accompanying this vision was a clear, audible voice in my mind. It said: "…tell him that the Russians will soon mount a mass attack and that you will get a bullet through the left leg just a hand width above your knee. The bullet will pass right through and will touch neither your knee nor any bone, nor artery, veins, nerves nor tendons. In fact, you will hardly bleed. Then you will be sent home for Christmas.

On your journey home, between Warsaw and the German border, the train will stop because the signal arm will be down. The orderly will jump out, cut down a small pine tree, put it in a can, and support it with stones taken from the railway bed. He will come back in and say, "… now, for us, it is Christmas!'"

After telling the Luxembourg soldiers what I had just experienced, the one who had asked if we would ever get home again retorted sarcastically, "No, my friend, you will get a piece of steel straight in your back, and by Christmas you will be a snow covered corpse."

I certainly didn't expect such a response and asked him if he was certain of this. "Of course not," he shrugged.

Two days later, the thunder of Russian artillery fire erupted all around us. Huge shells rocketed past to the left and right of us. War, once again, was very real. The good, peaceful times we had known on the Sozc River were at an end.

December 5th, 1943

The Russian Army broke through a hundred kilometers on both sides of us. We were ordered to pull back.

The next morning we moved toward the west. Just before entering the pine forest, I had one last, longing look back at that humble village. A thin blue stream of wood smoke still rose from our bunker. It drifted to a gray sky and an uncertain destiny. "Oh," I thought, "Mother Russia, I could love you, if only I could live here in peace."

*****

A Russian melody teased my mind. The Russian soldiers across the river sang this song on Wednesdays, in the evenings, after receiving vodka.

So, every Wednesday, after darkness fell, I was in the trench, listening as the air filled with their pleasant chanting voices echoing melodiously over the two kilometer wide swamp.

The leader's booming voice always started the others

off. These Slavic songs expressed some sad, sweet hope, poignant enough to inspire any soul. I prayed that I would never have to shoot any of them. As we moved westward, away from their camp, I realized, happily, that I would not have to face that challenge

By the end of the day's march we arrived at one of the many little, gray villages scattered about the countryside, and were able to get some winter clothing and some food. And not a minute too soon because winter had now settled in, and it was bitterly cold.

The next day we marched until noon, arriving at an unkempt and wild looking village. My Sergeant, myself and a fellow soldier saw an anti-aircraft division Major standing in his fine boots in the middle of the road.

My Sergeant was fearless and full of the devil and, about fifteen meters from this German officer, he bellowed out, "Why, look at this tango boy standing in the mud like a stork in a lettuce patch."

Taking offense, the officer shot back, "Hey you! What are you talking about? Stand at attention!"

Much to our surprise our Sergeant stayed calm as he hollered back,

"No, it is you who should stand at attention. The next time, you had better make sure you know to whom you are speaking!"

Of course, the Major didn't know what to make of it. He was no longer sure of himself. Our Sergeant might be an infantry General. By now we wanted to laugh out loud, but we didn't dare. Perhaps we had gone too far already.

Since we were wearing camouflage uniforms, all rank

distinction was covered. Still uncertain, the Major apologized as he moved away. And we made our way around the corner of the nearest house where we burst into laughter.

*****

We moved quickly on to the next town. Our Sergeant said his good-byes and departed on a four-week leave. He didn't know how lucky he was because we regular soldiers were quickly loaded onto trucks that provided for standing room only.

While the "Opel Blitz" rumbled along the dirt road, some of the soldiers started a political controversy. I disagreed with some of the statements and was dismissed as being too young and inexperienced to know the real ways of the world. I countered with the fact that I may have been considered young, but not too young to die for my country.

After awhile, some of them asked if I would share my cigarettes with them. I had plenty, because they were issued to each of us whether we smoked or not. Since I was a non-smoker I could have complied, but my feathers had been ruffled by the put-downs and I held my ground, becoming stubbornly mean. I refused their request.

The following day I regretted this foolishness because these men were no longer alive. I had acted out of pride and anger in refusing them, and to this very day I recall this bitter memory with deep remorse. If I had to do it all over again, I would have given them all my cigarettes. And even an embrace, because it would have been the last embrace they would ever get.

No, we are not born perfect, and must often learn the hard way in this journey of life. And I suppose we are still not perfect when we reach old age either, nor even when we die.

Chapter Three
In the Trenches

December 14, 1943

The trucks carrying us finally came to a stop around one in the morning. We were in a deep, dark forest. We were glad to arrive, finally, because we were starving and half frozen. A General standing on a box, holding a flashlight, greeted us with some kind of a welcome speech. He said he was expecting a mass attack later in the day and he wanted us to push our faces into the dirt because, he said, "It will be raining steel." He said nothing about food, drink or sleep.

It was bitterly cold that night. Fresh snow covered the ground. We moved to the edge of the forest, from where we could see our trenches. We couldn't advance any further because the Russians had bombarded our position with phosphor grenades, which was against international law. At night, it took on a burning, green sheen. Flesh and bone that came in contact with this chemical would burn, and slowly dissolve, causing great pain. An agonizing way to die.

*****

While we were sitting on fallen logs, waiting out the bombardment, some fell asleep, others smoked. I drew aside to be alone in prayer. It could well be my last one. I simply said: "Do you remember me, dear Jesus? I am the little boy who came to your church in Landau Pfaiz. My mama would like to give her son for her fatherland, but I want to live, and to return to her, because I still love her. I also want to see my motherland again. But, if I die here today, cold and hungry in the snow, I will love you still, and I will always love you."

I had my answer eleven hours later, and I will never forget it. My vision of December 1st became reality.

*****

Tired from our abusive journey, freezing from winter's cold creeping into our very bones, we managed only a few winks of sleep in one of the rough wooden bunkers scattered along the line. We were far from being in shape to meet tomorrow's impending battle. In fact, it was a good possibility that we might freeze to death before getting shot.

December 15, 1943

Morning came too soon. We arose with the first bright rays of sunrise. The sun shone brilliantly on six inches of new snow that fell during the night. You can't imagine how much I wished to be somewhere else. We knew that the tens of thousands strong Russian Red Army would charge directly against our defense line. They outnumbered us by at least two hundred to one. We didn't stand a chance. Still, we knew our duty, and we would defend our German homeland to the last man standing.

We had our meager breakfast of thin black coffee and unbuttered bread. This could be my last meal. I ate it eagerly, and with great appreciation. I still remember vividly the lukewarm liquid heating my throat as it trickled down and into my empty stomach. It gave me a surge of life that brought the blood leaping through my veins. Now, I was ready to fight!

As the sun slowly rose in the east, just beyond the Russian lines, I realized what an advantage it was to us. The advancing army would be unable to hide from us.

Our view ahead was clear for a good three kilometer stretch of open meadow, skirting a long, low hill silhouetted against the horizon. This was the Russian position of offense.

The sun on our dark uniforms gave us a little warmth. It even afforded me a few minutes of feeling good.

As the sun climbed higher we became aware of uncounted numbers of small, hammock-like objects, covered with snow, all the way, right up to the low hill, three kilometers away. We talked about it and came to the conclusion that all these small mounds were the makeshift graves of dead Russian soldiers.

Heaven must have had some compassion for this great sadness, because it had covered the frozen cadavers with a gentle blanket of fresh, soft snow.

We spent the morning repairing and improving our trenches. We had to keep moving in order to keep our bodies warm.

As I worked I was troubled by the perception that society is primitive and violent enough to ignore all the blood spilled and the rivers of tears shed because of wars. Why can't we learn that armed conflict doesn't improve people's lives. Except, perhaps, for the ones who plan the conflicts for personal, political gains.

I never trusted what we call human society, but right there and then it fell to the lowest level possible. And it has not risen a bit to this day. At this point in my young and difficult life, I had little knowledge of the Holy Bible. I thought, in fact, that I was somewhat negative. But then I read 1st. John: 2:15: "In him was life; and the life was the light of men. And the light shineth in darkness; and the darkness comprehended it not."

*****

At noon the Russians started an artillery barrage. It stopped thirty minutes later.

Then one of our men said: "They're coming!" I looked and saw the faraway, snow-covered hill turning black. They were coming indeed, marching body to body in a line two kilometers long, twenty to forty men deep. Thousands of men moved rapidly toward us, their first line firing constantly. Keeping our heads down as thousands of bullets rained down upon us, I thought that my last hour had come. With only a hundred men on our side to counter this massive attack, could any of us survive to see the sun rise the next morning?

There was a critical point when this black mass of attackers were only 400 meters away. In the terror of the moment, most of our men lost their courage. Nobody could expect to survive this.

At that moment my group leader and three men scaled the back wall of the trench and ran, but because of the steady rain of bullets fired by the first line of the attackers, they didn't have a chance. They all went down within seconds.

Now the machine-gunner from Luxembourg and I were alone. The only two soldiers left in the trenches. He pulled the trigger and I saw to it that the ammunition flowed. Every few seconds we changed position a few meters right or left and we never fired longer than in one to two second bursts. There were too many out there waiting to get us.

The firing at close range, with the Russians at the wire, lasted less than two minutes. The assault was over. The Russians turned and ran. I couldn't believe what we were seeing. We had given up hope of surviving. Now we looked at each other as if to say, "We made it!" But the danger was not over yet.

At this point a Corporal from our neighbouring unit came along the line. He was older than we were, with snow white sideburns. "Come on boys, we have to move fifty meters back or we'll all be killed!" he shouted.

He told us that the Russians had broken through the lines in spite of our efforts, and they were milling all around, trying to pick us off one by one. Seconds later we were shot at by a single Russian who was hidden twenty meters away on our right in a crater made by a grenade explosion.

At that moment, out of nowhere, an Asian soldier appeared. After the initial surprise of his abrupt appearance, I saw that he was wearing a German uniform, and that he was smiling at us. A Mongolian in a German uniform? This didn't make sense at all. Where did he come from?

He was carrying a German machine gun and had an expensive leather belt hanging loosely from his neck. Turning in my direction, and speaking with a heavy accent, he pointed in the direction of the grenade crater, saying that the Russian there was a big threat to us all. We should get rid of him. I agreed and, saying "Let's go!" I grabbed his ammunition box and we jumped out. We had advanced about ten meters when the Russian stood up. He fired one shot from the hip, hitting me in the left leg. I only felt a sting, similar to that of a small electric shock. The Asian asked me if I was hit. I told him I was. He then shot and killed the Russian. I jumped back into the trench and put two plasters over the two bullet holes. Normally a bullet enters a part of the body, strikes bone, and then spins and mushrooms. That is, it turns around and around inside the wound until it makes its way out after tearing a big hole in the flesh. Yet, by some miracle, this bullet did not mushroom. It narrowly missed the bone, and did not damage any blood vessels, nor hit any major nerve or tendon. There was little blood and hardly any pain.

One of my friends, a medic, directed me to a huge pile of hay where I found a doctor who administered a tetanus injection into my leg.

There were some thirty wounded men lying in the snow. Some were dying and others were moaning. The snow was bloody, and grenades were hissing over us.

A few minutes later the gunner who had been with me in the trench arrived with a nasty face injury. But he was smiling because now, he had a good chance to be sent home for Christmas.

The doctor, busy as he was, turned to us. "You two are in good shape," he said. "If you walk over this hill, then along the field road until you get to the rail line, you will find a barn where you will be taken care of."

We got up and off we went. I could still hear the doctor's last words: "You'd better move, because if they mount another attack we're all gone!"

When we got to the top of the hill, the Russians fired on us with an anti-tank gun. We took cover, then went on our way again. After awhile we arrived at a log cabin. There was no guard on duty that we could see, but we saw a red cross flag. We entered and talked to a doctor, who offered us bread, margarine and coffee. It was a feast!

In the next room two doctors, their white coats splattered with blood, operated on wounded soldiers. They were real heroes to work here, where armed Russians could appear at any time.

They suggested that we continue along this dirt road for two more kilometers, then we would reach the rail line.

We rested a while, drank a lot of water, and were on our way.

We arrived at the railway shortly before dark. We also found the huge barn we had been told about. There were some thirty wounded men on the straw. Here also was a lot of moaning. A single soldier cared for the wounded as best he could. He also had to dig graves, right in front of the barn. I could count nearly a hundred graves, all with crude wooden crosses, with helmets or caps on top and the soldiers' dog-tags nailed to them.

That evening I sat with the caretaker on a log beside the door. He told me that we would be picked up in the morning at 7 A.M. and that we would go by train to Warsaw.

We talked also about the mass attacks. This soldier had been there for a long time. He had talked to many people and had a lot of information. In the course of our conversation we came to the conclusion that Stalin's cruelty was inconceivable. He used the war to get rid of millions of undesirables and dissidents. He rounded them up, put them into uniforms and pushed them against the German Lines. How else to explain attacks of such magnitude, over sunlit snow fields, where ten thousand marched body to body, exposed to grenades and bullets over several kilometers.

Since Russia also had military strategists, such a battle situation could never 'just happen.' This was equivalent to planned murder.

The political commissars behind the columns were proof of the intent. They had orders to kill anyone who attempted to turn back. Perhaps the German gunners knew this and chose the commissars to pick off first.

Now I better understood what was happening, and I started praying for the Russian people. I am still praying. After 56 years, the suffering of the people of Russia was still so great that even if the whole world prayed only for Russia, it would not be enough,

I ended my conversation with the orderly with the understanding that, in case of an attack, both of us would do our utmost to protect the wounded. One could sleep for two hours and then go on guard for 2 hours. But there was no attack and with the morning, new hope was born.

16 December, 1943

It was still dark when the train arrived in the morning. At that time the locomotive engines were still steam driven. How welcome it was to hear that sound, with all the puffing and hissing. These were sounds from another world, another time, when things were peaceful and life was sweet.

By now my wounded leg had stiffened up, but I could still walk. The knee was only painful when I bent it.

I said goodbye to that lonely caretaker. I could go home and he had to go on with his grave-digging. All the wounded were carried to the train and placed on beds.

While the train gathered speed I had a good breakfast. There was plenty of food, since most of the wounded did not feel like eating. Now my only fear was that partisans might blow up the train with mines, killing everybody in it. It had happened many times before.

During the night we passed the town of Brestlitowsk. Some of the wounded died during the night. Although we were on the way to our motherland, it was certainly not a joy ride. There was too much suffering and pain riding in that train with us.

The orderly came to me to talk a bit. We were young and there was so much to talk about. We had a wonderful conversation.

17 December, 1943

When morning came we were rumbling into Warsaw. By now the orderly and I were good friends. But we had to part because the train stopped beside a huge hospital downtown. We were unloaded and examined within the hour. We were given a bath and brought to a good, clean bed. The doctor in charge told me that I would be treated in Warsaw, and that I would be back on the Front Line by January 15th, 1944.

If it was not God who gave me the vision that dark night on the Sozc River concerning my injury and homegoing, then certainly I would have to go back to the Front Line in January, 1944. However, if the vision really did come from God, then I would go home and the doctor would be helpless against divine power.

I slept for three days and refused all food. Then, next morning, a soldier in pyjamas woke me. He asked me if I wanted to go home to Saarbrucken, where my family lived. I answered, "Yes!" He wrote my name on a paper and told me to be ready at seven the next morning.

I could hardly believe my good luck, but I was afraid that the doctor might intervene, so I made myself inconspicuous by turning around and going back to sleep.

Chapter 4
Christmas

20 December, 1943

I only slept until about one A.M., to greet the new day. I remembered the importance of it. I was going home. I forced myself to go back to sleep.

At six A.M. I was awakened and offered breakfast, but I refused. I was too excited. The hour between six and seven A.M. passed very quickly. then, shortly after seven, I heard a commotion. Several soldiers with stretchers entered the room. A young man in pyjamas had the list in his hand. He motioned toward me. I crawled out of my bed and onto the stretcher, My leg was hurting now, and very stiff.

When I got on the train, I climbed into an upper bunk bed. For some reason I felt safer there. After a long wait the locomotive engine gave a signal. The train started rolling. Soon we were outside Warsaw and the train gathered speed.

The monotone sound of the moving train made me sleepy, but the moaning of the wounded men kept me awake, Many of them were not moving at all. Then there was a young man, just across the aisle, who was talking with his mother. For several seconds he listened, and then he answered. He said that it was not certain that he could make it home. His conversation lasted some thirty minutes and then he was quiet and never said another word.

The orderly came and asked me if I needed some medication. I thanked him for asking, but I had no pain at all now.

Two hours west of Warsaw, the train screeched to a halt. The orderly opened the window and saw that the signal was down. He opened the door, jumped out, and cut down a small pine tree. He placed it into a one gallon tin can. He then used some stones from the rail-bed to make it stand up. He rolled paper into balls and decorated the tree with them.

He stopped for a second to glance up at me. I was not more than four meters from him. He smiled, saying, "So, what do you think?" Looking at his work I said, "It's the best thing that I've seen in a long time! For us, it is Christmas!"

"Yes, sir," he said, "...and by the way, you are the only one around here who isn't dying. Nobody wants to eat. Hey! I have three sandwiches, coffee, and a half glass of gin. Would you want some of it?"

I told him that I had not eaten in three days, and that I would be happy to have it all. He brought it on a tray.

After eating all that, my strength came back, my stress level went down, and I felt like a million.

Now I had time to sit back and reflect. Suddenly my eyes filled with tears. I could see now that the vision that came to me in that dark night on the Sozc River became reality. The battle, the mass attack, the thousands of bullets that did not kill me, the one bullet that went right through my left leg to bring me home, the downed signal that stopped the train between Warsaw and the German border, the cutting of the tree, the tin can and the stones that held the little tree upright.

I had been saved again. Many of our soldiers had died, and others had run away. Certainly the Russians could have got past the barbed wire. They were only a few yards from us, and we two were only seconds away from being killed. But they turned around and ran. What could have frightened them enough to make them turn around? They were only seconds away from victory. If we had been killed, they could have marched unhindered toward the rail line, only an hour away, and cut off all train traffic to and from Warsaw. It would have been a catastrophe for all the troops further east, because they would then have been surrounded.

Yes, I was safe for now. But for how long? The war was not over yet. God might have to save me many more times.

The train rolled on, toward the west, passing many poor villages. Blue wood smoke rising to a gray winter sky. The orderly moved his chair near my bed and we talked for awhile about our lives. In the background we could hear the wounded moaning and murmuring constantly. As the train rolled on toward the west, where we all wanted to go, the living and the dead, the orderly moved down the isle, covering the ones that didn't make it.

When we arrived at a German border town, the dead were unloaded for burial.

We continued on our way, with half our original load,

toward a golden sunset. My only fear now was that the train could be bombed during the night.

In the gloom of the evening we passed through several bombed-out towns. The train stopped now and then, sometimes for hours.

We arrived near Frankfurt during the next day. In one of the little towns I saw a Christmas market in full swing.

24 December, 1943

When I awoke the next morning the train was following along a winding river. It was the Mosel River. All the slopes were planted with grapes. Some of the world's best wines are produced there. Now we were not far from our goal.

At ten AM we arrived in Merzig-Saar. We were transported to a huge, hospital surrounded by fields and wooded hills. It was beautiful. The sun was shining when I was carried into the hospital. This was the fulfillment of the last detail of the vision given to me in that dark night on the Sozc River. All of that was now so far behind me. But I would never forget it. Now I could sing, "Silent Night, Holy Night" in safe and friendly surroundings.

After a good, hot bath I was placed into a clean bed. There were three young nurses on the ward and everybody was in a festive mood. A red-headed patient from Bavaria decorated a majestic Christmas tree.

We had an excellent supper and enjoyed the company of members of a woman's organization. Later a group of young girls came by to sing Christmas carols.

When the lights were turned low in the evening I thanked God for all the blessings that had come my way. I also prayed for all the men on both sides of the Front Line who had to spend this holy night out there, hungry, cold, lonely and afraid, among thousands of casualties.

December 25, 1943

On Christmas day my parents and my two sisters, Martha and Gertrude came to visit me. Gertrude, with her girlish cheerfulness, saved the moment because emotions ran high and our hearts were melting. Still, we all managed to avoid tears.

After all, we were young and it was Christmas day. My father told me that on the same day that I was wounded my mother woke him up in the night because she had the feeling that something had happened to me.

There were no bombing attacks during Christmas time.

January, 1944

Brutal bombing raids continued anew as one German town after another was leveled to the ground.

By the second week of January I was allowed to walk around to reinforce my leg. I offered to help in the ward kitchen, washing dishes and serving food to the amputees. Because I was young, and not too badly injured, it was all great fun for me. The nurses appreciated the help, also, and begged the doctor to extend my stay. He did so, and the good times extended into March.

March, 1944

I was then granted a short leave, enabling me to go home for ten days. Between visiting, gardening and helping construct a bomb shelter, time passed too quickly. Knowing that the war in Russia would certainly come to a terrible end, I was reluctant to say good bye again.

The hour of departure came during a bombing attack, but Mama left the bomb shelter and came to the house to embrace me, and to see me off for, I thought, the last time. I know that she felt the same.

Looking back, I remembered that, at age four, I had said to my Mama that I never wanted to come into this cold world. Mama spanked me for saying that. Now, after all these years, I asked her if I had been so wrong with my childhood statement. She held back her sobbing only long enough to say, "I knew it too, but I did not want you to feel like that."

My father walked two kilometers with me from the house to the railway station while the air-raid was still on. When the train arrived, I kissed my father good bye and climbed aboard. I forced myself to go to a window and look out. The train started moving. My father looked up at me. Suddenly, he looked so old. We waved good bye one last time as the train picked up speed. I found a seat and sat there, sad and depressed. I didn't talk with anybody for hours.

We were almost in Berlin when a soldier called to me, "Hey, you, come on over here and talk with us. We're all in the same boat."

I was so thankful to him. He lifted me out of an aching aloneness. Soon we were all in a great mood and life was once more tolerable.

Five days later we arrived in Gumbinen, East Prussia, the most eastern province of Germany.

For two weeks I was assigned to serve in an honour guard. Every day trains arrived from the front lines. The dead soldiers were unloaded and buried with all military honours. Then we were shipped toward the front line again. Our only consolation was that we had the summer before us.

Chapter 5
On the Move

June, 1944

After a day in the train we were unloaded. A march of sixty kilometers brought us, finally, at the front line under cover of night. We moved into the trenches.

We could not dig the trenches to the proper depth because the ground water level was too high. This meant that we could never walk erect, not even at night, because the Russians were only fifty meters away and they had snipers with night-view glasses. They could pick off anybody who showed his head.

A few days later I was ordered to report to a battery of mortar and grenade throwers stationed four hundred meters behind the first line.

By now the Americans had invaded France. Fewer and fewer German soldiers were being sent to the eastern front and our troops were becoming more and more tired and depleted.

One day I was surprised to receive a package that bore my mother's handwriting. It contained a few affectionate notes and a wonderful cake that had turned into crumbs. But I ate those crumbs. Every one of them. They came from home. And from my Mama. I would have given all I had to put my arms around her. I kept the wrapping from this package for a long time.

July, 1944

A disabled Russian tank sat only twenty meters from our trenches. Sometime during the night a Russian soldier entered it, and when daylight came he fired point blank at us. The next evening one of our soldiers crawled to it with a powerful antitank mine. He placed the mine underneath the tank and attached a wire to it. When the Russian came back again and started firing, the mine was ignited, the tank and the man inside were destroyed.

When the dead man inside started to decompose in all the heat and humidity, there was such a stench of death in the area that we could hardly eat.

Early in the month we received orders to pull back because the southern and northern front were pushed back. While we were still holding the center front, the Red Army approached Warsaw. At this time we were still between the Djnepr River and the Beresina River and effectively cut off from food and ammunition.

About this time I was reassigned as a messenger to a Sergeant-Major. A quiet, intelligent man, he treated me as a father would, and we got along well together. Soon we were on the move, headed for Bobruisk. We had neither water nor food the first evening, and bedded down beside the road with a group of soldiers. Sleep was impossible because of the dense clouds of mosquitoes stinging us. Just as fatigue overcame me to the point of dozing, my Sergeant came searching for me among the soldiers. He came very close to me and said that the center of the German army was encircled by the enemy.

He said, "I want you to stay near me at all times. You are a good soldier and if we work together we can all make it to the German Lines."

The next morning we moved further toward Bobruisk and stopped behind a low hill. There was a village just over the rise that extended toward the Beresina River and the only bridge around to Bobruisk, which was on the opposite shore.

The windows of the village houses just before the bridge were full of Russian soldiers with machine guns and anti-tank guns.

We were told that we would attack the village at 10 AM. Because it was now only 9 AM, and I had nothing to do but worry, I decided to shave. I pulled my small packsack from my shoulders, found my brush and soap, dipped my brush into a puddle of water, placed my tiny mirror on the only surface around, a tank, and started soaping. I realized that we were in a terrible fix, but shaving was at least something to do. The tank commander opened a small shutter in the side of the tank, asking me, "What is it soldier, do you want to die freshly shaved?" I answered him that I was not expecting to die at all, The commander looked at me in disbelief, and the tank moved several meters uphill, firing into the village.

The crew of the tank had made their decision. They knew that they could never advance far enough to roll through the village and over the bridge. So they resigned themselves to do what they could, fight to the last bullet.

Anti-tank cannons hit the tank many times. It took four hours for the entire crew to be wiped out.

My Sergeant Major found a small earth bunker and suggested that we crawl into it to escape a mortar attack that was underway.

When our eyes got used to the dark we could see several women with children in one corner. They also were afraid of the mortar bombs. They were also afraid of us. Some were crying.

Then an anti-tank shell struck the roof of the shelter ripping it completely away. Now the women were screaming. We were half buried and sitting under the blue sky. It was a miracle that none of us were killed.

I decided to move away from the street level to lower and safer ground. When I was five meters from where I wanted to climb down, I was almost hit by machine gun fire. I dived to the right into a too small gravel hole. The bullets were still hitting the gravel just half a meter from my shoes. A soldier who had followed directly behind me threw himself on me. A third man did the same, but had no cover against the bullets. He was killed and his blood ran over us. We wondered how long we would have to stay in this position and how we could get out of it.

A few minutes later we had our chance. An armoured personelle carrier rolled past us. When it moved between us and the machine gun, we had scant seconds to throw the dead man off and run for our lives down the slope.

The deadline for the attack was postponed indefinitely. Toward five PM we tried to make a break through a swamp outside of the village. Two Russian tanks and a company of foot soldiers appeared to our right and started firing. They were on 300 meters from us. We were up to our knees in water. The bullets hit all around us, striking the water like rain. High explosive tank shells turned the swamp into a hell. I wondered why I was not hit. There were too many bullets to stay alive. The Sergeant Major was on my right side. Then suddenly he cried out over all the noise. "Hold it, we're not going one more step!" He pulled out his revolver, dropped to his knees, and shot himself in the head. He sank down into the water.

I was devastated. The only man I knew on that Front Line was gone. I really felt alone. The bullets were still hitting all around, but I did not care any more. I was in shock.

I moved slowly toward a wall of bulrushes. After I entered into this vegetation, the shooting stopped. Now that the noise subsided I could hear the screams of wounded and drowning soldiers in front of me.

The water was deeper now. It reached to my chest, but I could still move slowly forward over a floor of roots. Then it happened. My right boot entered the maze of roots and I could not get it out. I pulled hard, but I was afraid to get my left foot stuck, too. No, I did not want to die in this swamp. I moved my body horizontal and made swimming movements. With every stroke I pulled my right leg upwards. Little by little my foot got looser. Finally I could pull it up. I swam to a growth of willows and rested for a long time. Half of my brain searched for a way out, the other half had a conversation with God. Yes, the tank commander was dead, and I was still alive. But

I was in a bad spot and in a bad neighbourhood. If I only knew for how long I still had to swim. All I knew was that eventually I had to reach the Beresina River, and then swim over to Bobruisk.

What I did not know was that swimming across the river would have landed me in Russian occupied territory because the fast flow of the Beresina River would have carried me south.

I started to swim again, always toward the west, where the sky was still pink. Sometimes I rested, holding onto branches of willow.

Just before dark I lifted my face one more time to the evening sky. In the failing light I could see that I had arrived at a high ridge. Could it be a railroad that runs parallel to the river? I could see movement on top of the ridge. Then I heard voices. I feared that the men were Russians. If that were the case I would have to move around them in the dark in order to reach the river. I sank down so that only my eyes and my mouth were above water. Then I listened again. My heart made a leap when I heard some German words. Finally I left the water and climbed up to the top of the ridge. There I found nearly a hundred soldiers and a Lieutenant. I joined them. We now had to wait until dark to move over the bridge into Bobruisk.

Not far from us a railway car was on fire. It was filled with ammunition and shells.

When it was completely dark we moved slowly and silently toward the bridgehead. Nobody could foresee the outcome of this venture. If the Russians decided to shoot at the bridge, none of us would survive.

Because of my excellent night vision, I could make out a guardhouse at the entrance to the bridge. I could also see a barrel standing beside it. I walked over and dipped my hand into the liquid. It was beer! It did not bubble, but it was cool and good tasting. Because I'd had nothing to drink all day the beer not only gave me the liquid that I needed, but it also gave nourishment and relaxation.

I directed some of the men to the barrel and in no time it was empty. We finally made it across the bridge to Bobruisk. What we didn't know was that the town was encircled by Russians.

Over the next two days we found out that the road to the west was cut off by the Red Army. There was only one chance to reach the German lines. We would have to march north first, and then to the west.

On the third day we moved down to the shore of the Beresina then to the north. We were a column of about a thousand men. We were too many. It was not safe. The territory across the river was Russian occupied. It would take on one hidden tank across the river to cause death and destruction to our unit. Several of us separated from the others to move up to a higher level of the shoreline. There we saw a row of houses on top of the incline.

A couple of hours earlier I befriended a man who was a schoolteacher. He had told me that an end with terror would be better than terror without end. Suddenly a shot rang out from one of the houses. The school teacher collapsed and died. I dropped to the ground and directed some soldiers toward that house. They threw hand grenades in, and the shooting stopped.

I moved back down to the column and walked beside a Lieutenant. We walked toward the only tree along miles of shoreline. A shot rang out from the direction of the tree. The Lieutenant fell down with a head wound. Some soldiers looked up into the pine tree and fired several shots into it. Down came an old man with a long beard. He hit the ground with a thud.

Chapter 6
Captured

Several kilometers to the north we turned away from the river. We had to pass several houses on the way. We kept going, over a field with thick, dried up grass. When we moved toward a forest, the Russians were waiting for us. They got at us with machine guns and anti-tank cannons. A general, riding in a 4x4, his officers standing on foot boards around him, was blown away by an anti tank shell. Many died in a hail of bullets. Before we reached the forest the Russians had vanished.

It was very hot. In the forest we were glad to sit down in the shade. Three men sat with me at the foot of a tree. On my right were two soldiers who came from the same village. They sipped water from a dirty bottle and, because my mouth was dried out, I asked them for only one sip of water. They refused, explaining that the water was to be divided only between themselves. At that same moment a mortar shell exploded high up in the tree branches. A splinter of the steel mantel came down with a hissing sound and buried itself into the chest and lungs of the man sitting beside me. He coughed. His friend asked if anything was wrong. The wounded man did not answer. His friend lamented, "You can not die here and leave me alone. I will carry you all the way home." But the dying man said, "No, just leave me here and go home."

I left them there and went to catch up with the others. They were two hundred meters further ahead on the forest road. We settled down and waited until dark to proceed. A Sergeant Major picked out four infantry men as a rear guard. I was among them.

We were hungry and tired, so we sat down in the shadow of a tree.

The moon shone brightly. I fell asleep. Some time later, I woke up. By then we were all exposed to full view in the moonlight. At first the men looked to me to be dead, they were so still. When I tugged at their clothes, however, they woke up. We got to our feet very quickly and moved into the shadows. An hour or so later we had caught up with the troops.

We marched all night, taking a short rest at dawn, then continuing on our way. By noon we reached a village. I sat down on a wooden sidewalk with two other soldiers. I was on the left.

A shot rang out from the house behind us, and the man to my right fell forward into the street. Our situation looked hopeless. There were too many rings of the enemy encircled around us for us to be able to fight through. There had been one thousand of us when we moved out of Bobruisk, now we were less than three hundred. And there was hardly any leadership to hold us together.

Later in the day, while walking through a meadow, the soldier in front of me bent down and picked a handful of wild strawberries. Because I am colour blind, I had a hard time finding even one berry. Two more men came, and they each found several handfuls, while I was still searching for a second berry. They moved on and I continued to get a few more berries into my stomach.

Suddenly, an American fighter bomber dived at us, low to the ground, strafing with machine gun fire. Shots exploded to the right of me, and then to the left of me. The plane disappeared in the distance as I moved hurriedly into the forest. Here there was a gathering of some two hundred soldiers. There was a meadow in front of the forest and a village beyond that meadow. We could hear and see Russian soldiers in the village. There was also a brook nearby. Several soldiers walked toward it. I called to them to stop, but they ignored my warning and the Russians bombarded the forest with mortars. When the bombardment was over, most of the soldiers were dead, and many others were wounded. Cries of the wounded, pleading for help, followed me as I turned away, walking toward the west. They were beyond help now. There was nothing I could do for them.

I found one and a half slices of dry rye bread on the forest floor. Then I met a Lieutenant, all by himself, bent over a map.

I walked up to him and offered him half of the bread. He accepted it gladly. I asked him what his plan was. He did not answer for a long time.

Then he looked at me and in a low voice he offered me the best he could come up with. He suggested moving toward the west. We would have to cross a street, then swim across a river and try to find some food in a nearby village.

There was still a little gold colour left in the western sky, but there was no water and no food, and no place to lay our heads for the night.

Behind us were two hundred dead and injured, and in front of us only uncertainty. This part of west Russia was called: The Pripjet swamps.

*****

When dark descended over the forest, we moved cautiously forward, finding a path that we followed meter after careful meter. Sometimes we had the moonlight on us, and sometimes we moved into deep shadows. It was almost a ghostly atmosphere, cool and eerie. Because of the humidity

the spruce and pine gave off a strong perfume that reminded me of the forests in my homeland. But home was far away, and there was no time for such thoughts.

The path lead us in the direction we wanted to go, but I wondered who normally moved along it.

Because I was walking in the lead, I spotted a cord stretched across the path. It certainly was a device of some sort, waiting to be tripped. We crawled carefully underneath not to disturb it, stopping often to listen. But there was no sound except the occasional rattle of a machine gun far away, and the whine of the mosquitoes.

Suddenly, only two meters to our right, a man screamed and, in the German language, begged for his life. He had thought that we were Russians. The Lieutenant had a small flashlight. He illuminated two figures sitting on a fallen log. One was a German Corporal, and the other was a Russian in a German uniform. We told the German to be quiet. After a short conversation they asked us if they could come with us. We agreed.

Soon we arrived at a large field. We stopped. The moon illuminated the field and we discovered an outside bread-baking oven.

The place looked like a hangout for partisans, armed Russian fighters who operated behind the German lines. Then we heard a horse snort. We all dropped to the earth.

We asked the Russian in German uniform with us to call out in his language and ask who was there. He called out, receiving no answer. Now we knew that whoever was in front of us had to be German. We approached with caution, finding two German soldiers. One had lost a leg and was in bad shape. He was tied onto a small horse. The second soldier was the injured man's friend. We asked him if he wanted to travel with us, but he declined. He wanted to stay with his friend.

Much later in my life I learned that what lives on, after our body dies, is our loving relationship with God, and the love that we give to others, unselfishly.

We continued on our path. We were still thirsty and hungry, but we were also shaken by this event. Something had broken in us. Or, at least, in me. What a sad place this world is, where good men come to their end in a swamp forest infested with mosquitoes. Hungry, thirsty, badly injured and far, far from home. How many tears has God given to us to remember a scene such as this?

A while later we sat down to rest. We had to reach the road, and then swim across a river during the night.

It was around one in the morning when we saw, through an opening in the forest, the road, and a field beyond, well illuminated by moonlight. .

There before us was a whole army of Russians moving along that road. Men, trucks and tanks, all moving from left to right in front of us. There was no way we could proceed. All we could do was watch and wait.

A nearby big spruce tree, with thick branches hanging down to the forest floor, became our refuge. We crawled underneath those wide-spread branches and waited for the way to be clear. The flow of soldiers had to stop eventually, but before that happened, we all fell asleep.

In the early morning I was awakened by the Corporal. He was standing out in the open, calling to us, "Ivan is coming! Ivan is coming!"

I thought, what is the fool doing out there? but I crawled out to see for myself. When I stood up, three Russian soldiers were around me.

We were captured.

Chapter 7
Hell on Earth

What followed was so heart-breaking that it is difficult for me to write about it. There is so much pain in remembering the suffering, the loneliness, the hopelessness of those days. True, nobody was beating us, but we were without food and drink for so long already, and ahead of us the prospect of even more of the same.

I was prepared to die on the front line at any time, but being a prisoner of war was more than I wanted to endure.

I didn't even have a scratch on me, but did God keep me alive only to let me die in a slave labour camp? How long a future of hardship and starvation would there be before death came?

We were led to the edge of the forest. They ordered us to sit down. There were three guards around us. They inquired about our nationality. when they asked the Russian lad in the German uniform, he did not dare answer them. He was dragged into the forest and clubbed to death. In their estimation, he was not even worth a bullet.

In my estimation, however, he was a hero. He had the wisdom and courage to see that Bolshevism was a deadly cancer on the body of the Russian nation. He understood that his father, who had fought in the revolution for more bread and more freedom, was betrayed by Stalin, who not only killed the revolution, but also killed or starved millions of his countrymen.

While we were still sitting there, waiting for orders, a young red army soldier on a horse came by. He jumped down and told us to give up all our cigarettes, which he collected at gun point. Then a Russian Lieutenant arrived. One of our men, who spoke Polish, complained to the Lieutenant about the cigarette thief on the horse. The Lieutenant turned to the man on the horse, who continued lighting up his cigarette. The officer demanded that the cigarettes be given back to the prisoners. The soldier cursed and refused to comply with the order. He even laughed at the Lieutenant who, very cooly, pulled out his revolver and shot the foolish man from his horse. He emptied the pockets of the dying man and divided the cigarettes among us.

We were then brought to an enclosure, where we had to wait for two guards who would escort us back to Bobruisk. We were offered no food or water.

During the following hours of waiting I felt that God had certainly forgotten us. At the time I had no knowledge of the bible verse Matthew 10-38: "And whoever does not accept his torture stake and follow after me, is not worthy of me." This would have given me a lot of peace, and peace was what I most needed.

The two guards arrived and we started our treck toward the east. Although I had lost a lot of power in my legs, I was still strong enough to march in the front of the column, where we had less problem with dust. The soldiers who could not move any more were shot. Death was very close, and very real.

Thousands of Russian troops streamed toward the west. What could we do against such superiority in manpower? They could have fought on for another twenty years, even with great losses, with the help of American support, which, at the moment, they had.

All day long the passing Russian troops hurled insults and curses at us. Some even tried to run us down with their trucks. One Russian officer shot at us while driving by, but his bullet missed, killing one of the guards, who fell dead off his horse.

On we marched, in clouds of dust, in blistering heat, still without water.

Toward afternoon we saw a village half a kilometer from the road. The guard dispatched four men to bring back some water. They returned with full pails that were borrowed in the village. I could not see a way that the water might be distributed. Our soldiers were too thirsty. I didn't want to be the first to rush to the pails, but I decided not to wait too long. When I saw that twenty men rushed forward, I made a fast start and arrived before them. I pushed a 500 gram tin can right down to the bottom of the pail. When many hands and cans were pushed down over it, I stood right there until the pail was empty. Then I pulled my can out and had a full 500 grams for myself. What a joy to drink that cool water.

In the evening we bedded down beside the road in dusty grass. It turned very cool during the night.

At five in the morning we moved on. I marched beside

a friendly man with a good personality. I liked him, but I was concerned for him because he was in bad shape.

Soon we arrived in Bobruisk. We marched straight to the prisoner of war camp where only eight days ago Russian soldiers had been held.

When we walked through the door, several Russians rushed into the crowd and toward my friend. They embraced him and kissed him over and over again. Later I found out that he had been a guard in the same location and that he had shared a lot of bread with the Russian prisoners.

By now we were ten days without food. One of the men loaned me a small mirror. Looking into it I saw a tired, starved, worried and unshaven man. That sight vanished behind my tears.

After one night in that camp, we marched over the bridge spanning the Beresina River. There we were allowed to take a bath on a sandbar nearby. Every one of us drank a lot of water there, but it was not without danger because many bloated bodies were floating in the river. In some areas there were so many that they piled up behind the stone bridge pillars.

Soon we were on the road again, through that same village where we could not get through to reach the bridge just a few days earlier. We never saw anything to equal the number of bodies that were now strewn everywhere.

The Russians dug long, deep holes and dozens of political prisoners, armed with hooks, pulled the cadavers, one after another, to the mass graves, and kicked them in.

When we came up to the top of the hill, the land leveled

out. About a kilometer further we heard a commotion on our left. We lifted our tired heads and saw a village a few hundred meters away. We also saw about twenty people running toward us. We stopped. Men and women, armed with sticks and shovels, came rapidly toward us.

The Russian guard jumped from his little horse and called out to them to go back home. But they screamed louder, lifting their arms up in a threatening way. They came to kill us all. The guard called out one more time, "Stoy!" (stop!). They were only a twenty meters away and still coming. The guard leveled his automatic gun and pulled the trigger. Three persons fell to the ground. Now the villagers stopped. Looking in disbelief, they picked up their dead and retreated.

The stream of Russian troops and trucks so far behind the front line was never ending. The dust clouds rose to heaven. Some soldiers walked toward us to spit into our faces, others threw stones and some even fired directly into our column. Many of them shouted, "Dawai, na Vladivostok!"

It was hot. We were still thirsty and hungry. My mouth was so dry that my saliva had turned almost black. Toward evening we stopped beside a Russian field kitchen. We could hardly believe it. They gave us watery soup with shredded grain in it. A tiny flame of hope flickered in our hearts.

During the next day we finally crossed the bridge over the Djepr River.

From there we saw a train waiting for us.

Some 30% of us who set out to march east were no

longer alive. We arrived at the train and climbed up into real passenger coaches.

There was a tough looking man in my coach who claimed to be a member of the communist party of Germany. However, the communist party was forbidden in Germany at that time and there was no list of members. I hoped that he would survive his time in the Stalinist hell so that he could return to his land with changed political views. People flocked around him, seeing him as an enlightened savior. Still, he was unable to answer our questions.

I don't remember how we slept, or how long the trip took. Perhaps because by then I had switched my emotions off. From that time on I shed very few tears. If I was pushed, I slowed down. If I was left alone, I moved, but slowly. On this trip to Moscow we could at least rest. And we had water.

When we arrived on the outskirts of town we saw that great damage had been caused by the onslaught of the German army. We left the train and were marched to a huge horse racing track. We were, altogether, about fifty thousand men. We were divided into rows of ten, and were not allowed to get up except to go to the latrines, which were only big holes in the ground.

We were there for three days and nights. One night there was a big thunder storm. The rain poured down on us and we were actually sitting in the water.

At one point there were hundreds of soup kettles on wheels all around the race track. They all boiled water to produce steam. It looked so much better on camera. But we were never fed during the three days we were there.

Most of us came down with dysentery. The sick soldiers, and I was among them, were herded into open trucks which rolled eastward through Moscow.

We drove through a poor looking, rundown town. There were homeless people sitting and lying in the streets. Many of them were women. The surviving wives of soviet workers, no doubt, who should have been honoured members of the Bolshevik society. My heart was sore for these powerless, suppressed and tortured men and women.

Our truck rolled and rolled onward. In our truck there was standing room only and, because we all had diarrhea, it was beyond misery. After five hundred kilometers we finally rolled into Gorki, a town on the shores of the famous Volga River. The Volga was, and still is, the soul of Russia. There must be hundreds of songs, sagas, fables and poems about that river and the people along its shores.

We arrived, finally, at a hospital along a railway line. After a shower we received medication and were given real beds. I was placed in a hallway.

Just across the aisle, only a couple of meters away, was my nearest neighbour, Hans Joisten. He was a very well educated family man, age about forty. He came from Köln (Cologne). I sensed that he had the urge to talk, so I listened to him. He appeared to be very weak, and he must have feared that his end was near. Perhaps he did not want to die as "the unknown soldier," and saw in me a man to whom he could give his entire life history, and that I, then, could carry on with his story. It was clear that he felt that I was the only person in that big land of Russia with whom he could talk, openly and frankly, about his life. Over the next three days he told me about his childhood, about his first love, about his wife and children, and also about his shoe store. Now, all he had left of his life was the memory.

Because we were starving, he remembered all the delicious things he had at home. During his long stories, both of us were able to transfer our spirits back into our old world. Sometimes I had to remind myself where I was.

During the first week, three men from our ward died. Two weeks later we had to walk barefooted, in Russian underwear, through the center of town to a rail-line, to unload corn cobs.

After six hours of work, we returned to the hospital, tired and dirty. I brought with me a hand full of corn I picked up and hid in my pocket. I soaked the kernels in water, but they never softened enough to be chewed. So I swallowed them as they were. At least it was something.

Sometimes we were allowed to walk outside to get fresh air. There was a train station adjacent to the hospital. I watched one day as a train arrived, loaded to capacity with passengers. People were hanging onto the stairs, also, and even the roofs of the coaches were filled with people.

When the train stopped, the guard called out that nobody was allowed to sit on the roofs. Within minutes the roofs were cleared. A few minutes went by and as the train was leaving the roof passengers climbed back up from the other side of the train. The guard ripped his submachine gun from his back and shot several people down from the roof. The locomotive driver didn't even notice the shooting and kept on rolling. I couldn't believe what I was seeing. And I knew that I was truly blessed to be still alive in such a land where reason and compassion were unknown.

Over the following two weeks in hospital several more of our men died.

Chapter 8
Camp 185

September, 1944

When we left the hospital to set out on a twelve kilometer march we were first outfitted in coarse Russian clothing,

Toward evening we arrived at Camp 185, a huge forced labour camp. A five-meter high fence, constructed with sharply-pointed tree logs installed upright, enclosed it. A second fence of barbed wire was installed around that, and between those two fences German Shaped guard dogs ran freely. The camp imprisoned about eight thousand men.

As we entered the camp, the inmates were lined up for proverka (counting). That is, for a head count. Many of these prisoners had survived the famous battle of Stalingrad. Their faces were dull and resigned. Their skin looked like wet paper. Most walked with the aid of a stick. It was unlikely that these men could ever regain enough health to live normal lives.

We were all tired. The niceties of the hospital were over. Now I was staring into the ugly face of Bolshevism!

Our first meal came in the evening. It was a sample of the only food we would receive for the next four and a half years. It consisted of one slice, 200 grams, of dark, moist bread and 500 grams of watery soup. There was always some sort of unidentifiable matter sitting on the bottom of the bowl. Sometimes it might be vegetable peeling, or cabbage, or tiny fish with scales, heads and intestines. The soup we received that first evening had a foul smell.

I was sitting on a bunk bed beside Hans Joisten, the man from Cologne. I started to spoon my soup down. Hans didn't even start. He looked at me. I said: "Eat!" He answered, "I cannot eat that. It stinks." I argued, saying that if he didn't eat, he would die and never see Cologne again. He cried and pushed his bowl toward me.

The next day he was able to eat his soup. He looked at me with a degree of pride in his eyes. Yes, it was a victory for him. But it was his last one.

Work began next morning at 8 AM. Half of the eight thousand men were cutting lumber by hand with Swedish tree saws. The remaining four thousand walked eleven kilometers into the forest to carry out the trees that had been cut down the day before. All the lumber had to be carried out on our shoulders. We had to do that twice a day. Eleven kilometers in and eleven kilometers out. There were no trucks available for such work. All the American Studebaker trucks that had been received by the Bolshevik regime had been impounded for military use only.

The trees were cut to meter long lengths and burned in huge ovens to produce steam for several steam engines which, in turn, would run enormous generators for the purpose of supplying electricity for the whole district of Gorki.

The Bolshevik system could not work. The Soviet people didn't work hard enough to sustain themselves.

They lived under the whip. Therefore all basic necessities were produced by forced labour. The whole country was one huge forced labour camp, where workers earned only a starvation ration of food and nothing else. No freedom, no happiness, no privacy and no human rights. Certainly no religious rights. God was banned in Russia. What they did not know was that God was still there, but only for the downtrodden that loved Him.

In mid September I was among ten men who were chosen to work on an island in the Volga River, just two hundred meters from the shores of Gorki.

We lived in a shed that, years ago, must have been a storehouse. There was no insulation. The walls consisted of boards that were so dryad out that spaces gaped between them, allowing the wind to blow through. The floor was of the same quality. There were only three iron beds for ten men. We moved one bed to the left side of the room, the second bed to the center and the third bed to the right wall. Then we placed two long boards crosswise to the head end to support head and chest, two boards to support our hips and the remaining board at the foot end to support our feet.

We had no blankets, and, of course, there were no straw bags for us to sleep on. One kerosene lamp in the center of the barracks provided the only light.

That first night was so cold that we were only able to sleep for about two hours. We ended up standing in a circle around the one oil lamp, wondering how we could go on.

The next night was somewhat better because the temperature had increased. On the third night we each received a dirty old blanket. Every morning when the sun rose, we felt we had won a major victory. We survived the night. Our daily slice of bread and cup of watery soup further revived us.

One morning a Russian foreman led us to the south end of the island, where we pulled logs out of the water. We had to roll them into a horizontal triangle to give them a chance to dry out.

That evening I bedded down beside a man who was, I believe, about forty-five years of age. He came from East Prussia, the easternmost province of Germany. He was very lonely and depressed. One evening he moved closer to me and told me about his home. He said that he would be home for Christmas. I understood his hopeful day-dreaming, and did not ask him how he planned to go home.

During the night he walked along the shore and found a rowboat. He rowed straight across to the town of Gorki and was caught in the morning, while begging for food. He was thrown into jail. I never saw him again.

Some days we were picked up by a boat that brought us to the harbour of Gorki to load, or sometimes unload, freighters that brought goods to the town. For me it was a better occupation than pulling logs out of the Volga River.

One day at the harbour I had to bring a certain article to the operator of one of the boats. I walked up the plank and knocked on the door. When the operator opened the door I could see that he was frying eggs in a skillet. The aroma of these frying eggs brought a number of feelings and thoughts to me. I delivered the article to him. He thanked me and closed the door. I stood there, wanting to cry. I remembered my mother's kitchen and I had the feeling that I would die of starvation and never taste a fried egg again.

October, 1944

With the first snows of October we marched back to Camp 185 to carry logs again. It was freezing cold, and I was still walking in German army shoes, without socks or even rags to cover my feet. When I came back from the second forest trip that day, I had to pull my left shoe from my ankle. The shoe was frozen to the ankle. For several days I had permission to stay at the barracks When a doctor came and looked at my foot he thought that it was gangrene. Only then would they give me rags with which to cover my feet.

Chapter 9
Train to Siberia

1 December, 1944

Early in December the management of the camp prepared a list of those who would go on to Siberia. All my friends were on the list, including Hans Joisten, from Cologne.

My name was also on that list, but was removed because of the open wound on my left ankle that refused to heal.

I was alarmed. I didn't want to remain at Camp 185. It was really a death camp, where many died every week. I was convinced that Camp 185 must have been the worst camp, with the worst working conditions that the Bolsheviks had to offer.

I talked with the doctor and, after examining my wound, which had improved slightly, he added my name to the list again. Now I could look forward to going to Siberia.

This certainly might not sound right to anyone who had not spent a day in Camp 185. It was a camp where you could see young men bent over, walking with canes, like 90-year olds, their bodies and minds ravished by starvation and overwork. Many went insane, chewing on wood slivers all day and spending the night talking about food,

For a few days we still had to go to work in the forest. I remember one cold morning, with snow covering the land, I walked there with a long column of two thousand men trudging downward over a winding road. From my position at the end of the column, I had a startling view of those dark, tired and hopeless figures, slowly moving toward their goal, with pain in their bones and hearts, to vanish into the forest. If I live to be a thousand years old, I will never forget that scene.

Sometimes, memories of the Volga River came back to me. I would like to work along the Volga. Some boatmen were still pulling their boats along with long ropes, singing all the way. When I first saw that river, I was amazed about the mystic quality of it and the land along its shores. But I could never live there. Soon, in fact, I would be a thousand miles further east.

9 December, 1944

Finally we could turn our backs on Camp 185. Six hundred men set out to reach the railway, sixty kilometers away. We marched along a snowy road in our old army summer shoes. Our six guards were rude punks, barking like hoarse dogs. Hans Joisten was with us, although I had the feeling that he would never come back this way. I suspected that he had the same feeling. The most vulnerable age groups were age 20 or less and age 40 or more.

We marched all day, from morning to night. When we reached a village the guards led us into a small theater. The first thing we saw was a portrait of Stalin. The face was six meters high, and the mustache must have

been two meters wide.

Inside the theater we all sank to the floor and fell asleep within a few minutes. There had been no food or water after a thirty kilometer winter march. I woke up during the night and asked the guard sitting in the only doorway if I could go to a toilet. He answered me with a curse and told me to go to hell. I did not go to hell, I went to the stage and entered through the prompt box, or soufleur. There, under the floor of the stage, I found several other men urinating. So I joined them. My problem was solved. Next morning, on the way out, I imagined Stalin pulling his nose up in disapproval.

We were soon on the last stretch to the railway, with neither soup nor bread. We looked forward to getting inside a cattle car, where we all could stretch our tired bones on some straw on the floor. Maybe there might even be a stove inside. They would certainly have to feed us right at arrival or we could not last much longer.

There was a small man marching in front of me. He obviously had difficulty staying on his feet. A short distance down the road he fell. We lifted him up. Soon, he fell again. I remembered the torturous road Jesus had to walk. It was illustrated on a painting in my church with the wording:

"And he fell the second time."

Yes, this man made it to the train alive. At that moment he might have had a flicker of hope, but he did not leave the train alive.

The last ten kilometers to the rails was absolutely

straight. Anyone looking down this road could believe that it would never end. After a long time, there was an opening and a bend to the right.

When we arrived at the bend, just before the waiting railroad cars, we saw a very old couple standing on the left side of the road. The man had a long beard. Both were poorly dressed. Like all the people in this land. Both were bowing to us and calling out: "Scora damoi, scora damoi" (You will go home soon).

The guard, adding some curses, told them to shut up. But the two old people kept on bowing. The old man was crying. They did not bow because we looked like royalty, they were bowing in front of so much suffering. They obviously were no strangers to suffering themselves. The humility and compassion of these people touched me deeply. They endured humiliation and took time to give us hope. I thought there and then that the people of Russia were ultimate sufferers. I have prayed often for this old couple.

Shortly after, we arrived at the train. There were eleven cattle cars, and a locomotive. Each car took sixty men. There was a small wood stove in each car, but no wood. There was also a ten inch round hole cut out of the oak floor to be used as a toilet. There was no straw on which to sleep. We had boards to sit on, but sooner or later we had to lie down on the icy floor to sleep.

The guards closed the doors, yelled back and forth some more, and after a while the train started to roll.

We were not told anything, but we all hoped that the journey would be westward. We looked through cracks between the boards to try to find out in which direction we were going. We speculated that perhaps the Russians were moving us nearer to the German border because they could see that the war was coming to an end?

But, pleasant surprises never happen in the Soviet Union. The train gathered speed and an icy wind blew a cloud of snow up the toilet hole. We took one of the sitting boards and covered the hole with it

By now we knew that the train rolled eastward. Nobody wanted to say it, but it was clear that our destination truly was Siberia.

The nights were terrifying, and long. Darkness, cold and hunger. It was a misery such as we had never known. None of us were certain to see the morning light.

One of the men was a hotel owner from the town of Wiesbaden, not far from my home. He talked for days about what kind of food he served in his home. He certainly had seen better days. One day he got really restless and ran head first against the door, screaming, "They're coming, they're coming, with food and water!!" But nobody came, of course. We talked to him and quieted him down. He became calm, and cried. In the morning we found him dead. He did not have to suffer any more.

The train took fifteen days to reach Siberia. During the journey I did not count days or hours. With one slice of bread every third day, and some water every second day, all we could do was survive. Mentally and physically. Some days not one word would be uttered by anyone all day.

*****

Somewhere between Gorki and Kazan the train stopped to take on coal and water. During this stop we had the only genuine pleasure of the whole journey to Siberia. We were told to disembark and stand in line in front of the steam engine. The engineer looked out his window at us, pulled down a lever, and hot water spurted out of a pipe. He directed us to hold our American tin cans underneath the jets of water. We could each have five hundred grams of hot water. To me, it tasted like chicken broth.

I wonder what that engineer felt, deep down in his heart.

Several days later, I lost another friend. He was a quiet, friendly man from Celesia. During the evening he came near to me and whispered. "They took my flesh, but they'll never get my bones!"

When our bread ration arrived the next morning, I handed his slice to him, but he did not take it. At first I thought that he was still asleep. He was in a sitting position, with his back against the outside wall. Then I looked at him more closely in the dim light of the car. I saw then that he was dead.

And frozen.

When the train stopped near a village, the guard pulled the dead man out, stripped him naked to sell his clothes for vodka. He then threw the naked body into a snowy ditch beside the railway.

Every second day one man from every car was escorted to the first car behind the locomotive. A Corporal, the leader of the guards, then counted sixty slices of bread into a sack. The guard then escorted the man back to his coach, but on the way the guard took for himself as much bread out of the sack as he could stuff into his uniform. That bread was then used to pay for more vodka at a village along the railway.

One man, who wanted to bring all the bread back to the coach for the prisoners, resisted the thief and was roughed up by the guard. Consequently, the man brought back even less bread. He cried, and asked God to end it all.

It was bitterly cold. The train rumbled on. We felt it rolling over a bridge that spanned the main street of a town. Looking through the cracks, I could read the name of the town. We were now in Kazan. How I would have loved to ride in a streetcar again, under normal circumstances.

Several days later we had the sensation that the train was climbing. We were on the western slopes of the Ural mountains. The Urals divide Europe from Asia.

A lot of fresh snow lay on the ground. I pulled the cord I used as a belt out of my trousers, and fastened it to the wire handle of my five hundred gram tin can. I took the board off the toilet hole and lowered the can slowly into the fresh snow. When I pulled up the filled can, four men wanted to fight for it, but I covered it with my hand, and pulled it under my body while I was kneeling beside the hole. I told them that I could get snow for everyone, but it had to be done slowly and carefully. Everybody agreed and we all ate as much snow as we wanted. At least we could get some water into our bodies.

The next day we were high up in the Urals. It was very

cold. How could we survive such conditions? Nobody talked about our chances of survival. How much longer?

Ever since we entered the cattle car I squatted on my haunches, leaning with my back against the closed north door. Suddenly, at mid-morning, the big door on the south side toppled out. It fell into deep snow. We were already in a horrific situation because of the extreme temperature. This made matters much worse. If nothing could be done we were doomed to freeze within the hour. The guards were unaware of the incident. Everyone in the back of the car rushed to the other side to escape the icy wind.

Necessity found some sort of a solution. We leaned all the sitting boards vertically in front of the opening. Then we took our coats off and did our best to close off the remaining hole. If the door I had been leaning against had fallen out, I would have fallen out with it. Even without injury I would have watched the train disappear in a cloud of snow. With villages and towns hundreds of kilometers apart I wouldn't have had a chance. I would have frozen my feet in no time because of the summer shoes I was wearing. I would have had nothing to do but say my last prayer and sit down and die. But I had a very loyal and powerful friend, and that made all the difference between life and death.

It was afternoon when the train finally stopped. A guard walked along the train's length and discovered that the door was missing. He climbed up into the car with an iron bar in his hand. He was intoxicated. He herded everybody into one corner. He had to count us and motioned to us to come forward one at a time. He held the iron bar in his two hands, ready to hit whoever would walk past him. He said: "Dawai adin" (come on, one.) I was standing right in front. I knew that it was a dangerous situation. I walked forward and when I saw that he was lifting the bar, I dropped to all fours and galloped like a dog to the other corner. He was more than surprised. He found it so amusing that he shook with laughter. He said: "Ojin carasho" (very good).

The second man came forward. It was the little soldier who fell twice on the march to the train. The guard hit him in the back with full force of the iron bar. He fell down. The next day, he died. Now nobody wanted to come forward. Then the brute leaned his iron bar against the wall and we knew that nobody else would be hit and the counting could be completed.

Slowly the train descended the eastern slopes of the Urals.

We arrived in the town of Swerdlowsk, a mining town. Everything was black and run down. It looked like a town with no joy and no energy. All the effort went to the state and nothing was left for the people. It was plain to see that the love of Moscow was nonexistent. There was no hope here.

We were led to a factory shower. It was a dark place. The windows were filthy. There were many stalls, but only a single pipe overhead, with a single hole through which a trickle of luke warm water fell. We could see that the Soviet workers were far from spoiled.

I washed quickly so that I had time to drink the water. There was, of course, no soap or towel.

I noticed that most of our men had swollen legs. Many of them had open and bleeding wounds.

As dirty and sad as Swerdlowsk was, it was better than our train, where about sixty-five men had died already, and the rest were weakening fast.

The train pulled out in the evening and we began the slow descent downwards, into Siberia.

Going down the slopes into this endless land gave me the desolate feeling that we were now truly forgotten. Mankind would not remember us. Life was at an end. All that awaited us was work, hunger, cold and death.

Nobody knew that I was here, and nobody would be able to hear my cries or my last sigh. Nobody on earth could help me. I knew that my loved ones prayed for me. But they were far away. The winds of the Urals blew away my past as we rolled down into a land to which I did not belong, and where I was a nobody.

But God said, "You ARE somebody. You are my friend. I am still here, and with you, to love you and protect you. How many times do I have to prove to you that I am with you? When you have nothing left but a sigh, I will be there to lift you up. And I have the power to work out a recovery for you. And I will give you your youth back, and you will be a mountain of faith that can not be shaken by any storm." What could I say? I said... Amen.

Chapter 10
The Barracks

24 December 1944

It was Christmas Eve when we arrived at our destination. Sunny, but bitterly cold. The train slowed, then stopped in early afternoon outside the town of Tyumen, district of Sibirskaya.

The door opened I watched as the men jumped down. There was no unloading ramp. Most fell into the snow, but were unable to get up. Soon a hundred men from the nearby camp came over and lifted the weakened men up and carried them into the camp.

We were then directed to the banya (boat house). The door was opened and the first man to enter could not climb a thirty centimeter high step.

Two Romanians came to help each man as he entered. We received about two liters of warm water. It was too little, too late for some. We enjoyed the warmth on our cold bodies, but two of the men collapsed and died right there.

We were then led to a barracks and allocated bunks. We were also issued warmer clothing: Sheepskin coats, hats, gloves and felt boots that came up to the knees. Evening came. We received our soup and bread. It was the same quality of watery soup and the same amount of bread as in Camp 185. Now we knew that as long as we could survive here in this land, this would be our only sustenance.

Nobody spoke. The situation was grave.

The camp commander paid us a visit. He said that we would not go to work right away because of our weakened condition.

At about 8 PM one of the men asked us if he could sing Silent Night, Holy Night. But nobody wanted to face a song like that now. Those among us who still had the strength to think, turned their thoughts toward home. Many moaned and many died right there and then on this holy night.

After awhile the young singer offered to sing a love song for us. It was a song, he said, that he used to sing with his mother at home. We agreed to listen, and for the most part we enjoyed the song. The young soldier who sang for us died soon after. His mother will surely miss him.

25 December, 1944
Christmas Day

We were all told to come outside and stand in line. Many of the men had to be assisted. We did not know why we had to stand there in such freezing weather. The thermometer on the entrance to the guard house registered 40 degrees below zero.

The camp Commander then arrived and apologized for calling us out. The six guards from the train were also there. The Commander asked us why we were so weak. Some of the men pointed their fingers at the guards, explaining that they stole our bread and with the proceeds bought vodka at the villages along the rail line.

The Commander turned and hit the guard Corporal in his face. He then ripped the shoulder straps from all six guard soldiers, dismissed them from the army on the spot, and condemned them to five years hard labour.

We were stunned. Now we knew that there could be a measure of justice in the Soviet Union.

January, 1945

The barracks was dim inside. In our hearts, it was dark, also.

The barracks neighbour to my right was a burly, friendly man. He was a baker from the Saar country. He suffered from acute tuberculosis. He knew that nobody could help him. There was no medication and no additional food. He had a smile, though, that said: Look, soon I will be at peace. He died two weeks later in his sleep.

Toward the end of January it was still bitterly cold. The humidity froze on the inside of the small windows to a ten centimeter thick, yellowish ice layer. Light could scarcely filter through. We were allowed only five logs a day to burn.

Two of the barracks at this camp were filled with prisoners who were incapacitated by starvation and sickness. A third barracks was filled with about a hundred men who were beyond saving. Most of them suffered from tuberculosis, edema, heart disease or general weakness of all organs.

There was also housing for the ones who were able to work. And a kitchen, an instruction barracks and the bath house, with its delousing facility.

Throughout the month of January I sustained a high temperature.

Every week a female army doctor came to check us out, but she had no medication to work with. One by one we had to get up and sit naked on a chair three meters across from the doctor. This lady doctor was Jewish and about forty years old. When it was my turn to sit in front of her, she asked me why I was sick. I answered that I was not sick, that I only needed more food. She nodded and forced a smile, but the tears were running down her face. I must have looked terrible. Or she might have a son my age. I weighed about forty kilos. I had only bones left. They were covered by yellow-brown wrinkled skin.

Sometimes we were moved around in this barracks, or sometimes we took our blanket and moved by ourselves to another bunk. Most of the time, in winter, I wanted to be on the upper bunk, but in summer I preferred to be on the lower bunk.

One time I was bedded down between two friends. The man on my left was twenty years old. He was from Wesfalier. He was a very nervous young man. On my right was an older man, about forty. He came from Celesia. He talked quietly and deliberately. Everything he said was thought over first, before being spoken. He had no hope and no courage. He suffered from edema. His kidneys didn't work properly. His legs were like stove pipes and the edema had reached his intestines.

The younger man had tuberculosis. Both men were convinced that they would never go home again. The two of them talked often, sometimes involving me in the conversation. I can still see the face of the older man. He was near death and without hope, but his brain and his emotions functioned normally. At this time, I had malaria. Every day, toward noon, I felt like ice, and an hour later I would have a high fever. I figured that I had a good chance to die early.

But these two men had a plan. One day they decided to buy rock salt, which blocks the kidneys, thus hastening death. They traded tobacco for rock salt, and within three weeks both had died.

About two weeks after my malaria subsided I had a second bout with dysentery. There was no inside toilet in this barracks. The outhouse was thirty meters away in the bitter cold. Because many of us could not make it to the outhouse, they placed a barrel outside the door. One day I had to go to this barrel fast, but I did not quite make it. Sitting on that dirty frozen barrel outside, in plain view of passing people, I soiled my only cotton pants. I had to get up fast from my seated position in order not to freeze to the barrel. There was, of course, no toilet paper. This was Siberia.

Not knowing where or how to clean my pants, under the circumstances, was one of the most humbling experiences of my life.

We did have a water tap inside the barracks, where I washed my pants and my legs with icy water. Then I had to put those wet pants back on. I then rolled myself into my only blanket hoping that it all would dry out.

After the sixth person beside me died of tuberculosis the Russians were convinced that I was the carrier of this disease, remaining immune to it myself.

In order to find out if I was the carrier, they brought a horse and sleigh, placed many blankets on it, placed me on it and covered me with many more blankets. They were to take me to town for x-rays. The horse ran all the way. I prayed that God would make the signs of tuberculosis show up on the x-ray. It was the only way to get home. Yes, I was dying. but I wanted to die at home, beside a stove, with enough water to drink and enough bread to eat.

Somewhere the horse was reined to a stop. I climbed an outside stairway to an upper floor. There I met two doctors in white coats. They had a very civilized appearance. I thought that I was in a different world. They took a look at my lungs and told me that my lungs were healthy.

I cried all the way back to the barracks and asked God: "Why, why, why?"

Today I know why. Because I needed my lungs for a long, active life.

When I arrived back to my bunk in my barracks my neighbours told me that my friend Hans Joisten had died. That was a devastating blow.

Two weeks later I came down with pleurisy. My back ribs were very painful. Several times during the day the blonde nurse, Lisa, came to look after me. She liked me, and always did a little more than she had to do to make me comfortable. She had no medication, or other resources, so all she could give to me was caring.

A few days later I was really dying. I lay on my belly and knew that my life force was draining out of me. I could not move any more. I could not even remember home.

They called Lisa and I heard her say, sorrowfully, "Oh, Scherer is dead." She sat for a minute on my bunk, then she left and came back with a white linen cloth that I believe was her own. She covered me completely, to give me more privacy.

But had God not saved me through many other battles? Did he not say that he had the power to lift me up after my last sigh? Well, now was the time for him to act, or it would be too late. But how would he accomplish this?

It was eleven in the morning. One hour before the food was to be brought in. My right neighbour bent over me to talk to my left neighbour, saying that they should not report anything about my death until they had taken my food for themselves. They intended to do the same for the evening meal, and report my passing only in the morning.

My inner voice said: "Get up, didn't you hear what was said? They want to take your last meal away from you. Get up and prepare to eat your last meal!"

With that, I pulled myself up. It was so painful. My legs and arms did not function any more. I had no power left. I held myself up by embracing a wooden corner post. There were cracks in that post that were full of bedbugs. They hurried out to sting my face.

One of my barracks mates brought nurse Lisa back. She was surprised that I was still alive. She hurried out and came back with a big cup of black tea. She told me to stir it. She had put two soupspoons of impossible-to-get sugar into the tea. There was no tea or sugar in the camp kitchen. It had to have come from Lisa's own belongings. After drinking this heavenly stuff I felt much better. My heart beat more strongly. The crises was over.

Two months later I could walk outside in fresh air and feel the promise of spring.

Chapter 11
Camp 2

May, 1945

Early in May, as I walked along the wooden sidewalks of the camp, I met Jupp Kinauer a disillusioned Communist who was in charge of work to be done inside the camp. At that moment all the sirens of Tyumen went off at the same time.

Because it was only eleven in the morning we couldn't understand why the sirens were going. We strolled together to the gate and asked the Corporal there why the sirens were sounding. He told us that Germany had capitulated. We turned and walked back, each of us troubled in his own way. I looked at Jupp to see how he was taking it, and I saw that he cried. The German Communist Kinauer cried! I embraced him, to comfort him, but he said over and over: "These animals won the war." (Meaning the Bolsheviks.)

June, 1945

The Malaria was back. Every day, at exactly eleven thirty in the morning, I was freezing to the extent that my teeth chattered. They placed several more blankets on me, then at twelve thirty the fever started. After an hour, the fever went down.

Malaria kills millions of well-nourished people every year. Since I was already a skeleton wrapped in skin, only God could keep me alive.

The fever came back every day for a week. As soon as the malaria was over I felt much better and after four weeks I went to work for the first time since December, 1944.

Russia, at that time, had no transportation so we were delivering all kinds of materials. Early in the morning we marched down to the Dura River where a boat brought us to the harbour on the opposite shore.

On this particular day we were to unload a boat filled with bags of American flour weighing 60 kilos each. They were heavier than we were. A harbour master showed us the trick of how to carry these bags. They had to be carried across the back of the neck, balanced between both shoulders. then it was another balancing act to get them up the gang plank to the quay, then up an incline and into the store house.

Because we were very hungry we ripped a bag open and ate some flour. Our guard saw it. He placed the open bag in the center of the store house and each time a man brought a bag up, he was entitled to take one spoonful of flour. The dry flour was not easy to swallow. Sometimes we almost suffocated.

And the swallowed flour in our stomachs screamed for water. There was no water tap from which to drink, so we walked down to the river. Before we could drink, we had to push the scum and debris away. This debris consisted of straw, wood planks and even human excrement that came from the boat people. The water I drank was the color and consistency of pea soup. While I was drinking I thought that if I could survive this, I could survive anything.

A few days later we unloaded a ship that carried a cargo of salted fish. The fish were brought to the storehouse and dumped on the floor. When we were certain that nobody watched, we grabbed a fish and took a bite out of the neck, which is, most of the time, bone free.

Another day we unloaded bags of American sugar. It was hard work for men in our condition but somehow we always got a little something out of it to nourish our bodies. We were not thieves, but we needed to survive.

While we were working at the harbour, one of my friends, a blue-eyed young man, with a bad stomach, came to me all excited. He showed me that he had found a barrel filled with alcohol. Somebody had drilled a hole into the oak wall. He said, "Have some, it's good for you." I dipped my finger in it and tasted it with my tongue. I found that it was too strong. I discouraged him from drinking any of it because it could only be bad for his stomach. But he said that he had a few spoons of it and that he felt well.

When we got on the boat to be taken back to the barracks, I noticed that several of the men had fallen asleep. By the time we arrived on the opposite shore, four of the sleepy men could not get up. They had to be carried to the camp, where they died. Among them was my blue-eyed friend. Later that same evening, four more men died.

One of them had arrived at this camp only three months earlier. When we were all standing near the door to have a look at the newcomers, the man beside me rushed forward and, with a great shout, embraced one of the newcomers. It was his brother! They had fought in different divisions on the Front Line. Now they were meeting each other again, in Siberia, thousands of kilometers from home.

The man who had rushed forward to greet his brother with a shout, was the healthiest man in the camp. Nobody could understand how he could look so healthy, and how he could be so strong. And yet he was one of those men who died that evening. His surviving brother was devastated.

July, 1945

We assembled in the camp yard for the last time. We were preparing to leave Camp No. 1 and move to Camp No. 2, a short march of a few kilometers along the shore of the Dura River.

We set out, never looking back. Our stay there was the most difficult time I had ever lived through. Several times, I nearly died, and I lost many friends who would have liked to march out those gates with me in the hope of starting a better life somewhere else.

The day was beautiful. Hot and dry. Walking toward Camp 2 we passed the entrance to the bridge that crossed the Dura River toward the town of Tyumen.

I walked beside a man from Celesia. His name was Hans Lamer, and he had an agreeable personality. I can still see the droplets of sweat on his smiling face.

Camp 2 was located beside a huge plywood factory. We were allowed to rest for the afternoon, so we stretched out on our bunks and had a little conversation. Hans told me that he was a hotel cook by trade. We were on the verge of falling asleep when the door opened and someone called out that Hans Lamer should come to the kitchen. He grabbed his belongings and left.

At Camp 2 we had two big barracks buildings for the men to sleep in. The third one was made into a kitchen and an eating place with tables and benches. I hesitate to call it a dining room because nobody dines in Siberia. Besides, a dining room is not a place where rats run around.

The bath house was two kilometers down the road. We were allowed to wash ourselves only once a month with two liters of water each. Most of Camp 2 worked in work brigades, and most of the work had to do with plywood fabrication. The logs were cut in the Ural mountains, many hundreds of kilometers away. They were thrown into a river and floated to Tyumen. Then they were pulled out of the water and cut to about one and a half meter lengths to fit the machines. The logs then had to be transported to the factory.

A Romanian engineer had built an electric train to transport the logs. When he died, the motor could not work any more. The angry Russians threw the engine and all the cars from the rails, and just let it rust there. Then we had to do the job the Siberian way. We rolled the logs with the help of steel rods one and a half meters long with a hook on one end and a handle on the other. It was an excellent tool, but not meant for industrial use. These logs had to be rolled every day of the year, summer and winter. A man had to roll a log ten meters, then stepped over it and let the next man take over and so on until the log reached the factory, where the bark was stripped off. Then the logs were boiled in a huge vat to prepare them for cutting for the production of plywood. .

Rolling logs for eight hours was difficult enough because of the monotony of the job, but even worse because of the extremes of heat and cold. The night shift was like rolling logs forever. The nights seemed never ending, partly because the only illumination for the job was a 60 watt light bulb every one hundred meters.

October, 1945

The food in Camp 2 was the same as everywhere in forced labour camps in the Soviet Union. It was still only three 500 gram watery soups each, and three slices of dark, wet bread, the weight of which depended upon the availability of flour.

There was absolutely nothing else to eat or drink. Even tap water was not provided in any of the thousands of slave labour camps in Siberia, and throughout the rest of Russia.

We each had only one blanket to cover us at night. The outhouse was always far enough from the barracks to make it difficult for a walking skeleton. The number of survivors went down at a steady pace.

There was a cabinetmaking shop within the plywood complex. Four of our men worked there, but one of them became very ill. I was offered an opportunity to take his place.

Within the week I produced four book shelves per day, which was a 100% increase in production. After one month I was able to produce six book shelves per day. I liked the woodwork much better than the log rolling. The Russian management nailed a 4 x 8 sheet of plywood to the wall, with my name on it. They honoured me as a good worker. They put this announcement up just in time for their October revolution day. But it was all only words. There was not to be one additional morsel of bread.

I worked inside now, but to my surprise, there was no heating in this shop. When December came we were freezing and, since the glue was water based, we couldn't glue things together. Now everything had to be nailed. The nailing was done with homemade nails that looked like hoof nails, 1924 style.

The manager of the work shop at this time was a Jewish man. When the Russians advanced into Poland, Mr. Frankel was picked up and brought to Siberia. His wife and daughter could stay in Warsaw. He told me that he could escape death by starvation only by selling his wedding ring. All he had to look at to remind him of his family was this ring, but he had to part with it. The fact that he told his bitter story to me, a German prisoner of war, showed how painful it was for him.

He had studied at the University of Leipzig, Germany, where he lived through the best times of his life.

There were many power failures during the night. All we could do was to sit down in the dark and wait. On one such occasion Mr. Frankel came away from his counter and sat beside me on a pile of plywood. While he was talking about Germany, he asked me if I could remember the wonderful coffee houses, with all that fantastic pastry. I told him to talk about something else, or I would cry. But he laughed and went on talking about his good times and good food.

One morning Mr. Frankel came in smiling. I asked him if there was anything to smile about. He said, "Yes, for me. I received the travel documents from Moscow, and money from my wife. I will travel to New York. I will move out of Hell now!"

I was so happy for him I put my arms around him and wished him all the best in his future. Then he did not smile any more. He left a few minutes later. We waved at each other. It was hard for us to see him vanish through the door. We were all still there, in this rat infested, cold factory, not knowing if we would ever be able to leave and go home.

In the morning we had a new manager. He, also, was a Jewish man. I asked him if it was possible to turn the steam heating on because it was 30 degrees below zero, even inside. He said that the heating unit had been rusted for twenty years. Nonetheless, I begged him to try to turn it on because it was almost impossible to work. He turned the steam on and within minutes nobody could see anything any more. The hot steam and the low temperatures created a dense fog. We could move only with our arms stretched out in front of us.

I know that many people in the west will have a problem believing the situation in the Soviet Union. All the speeches addressed to the Russian people were empty words. The incredible poverty of the population did not reflect the promises that came out of the politicians. There was not enough food, no new clothing, no new housing, no new factories. Everything was old, old, old.

I never saw a construction site; the windows of factories were blackened by decades of neglect. Whatever the land produced, and it was very little, went to the army or into prestige matters to keep the shell of the masquerade in place. There was nothing behind all the trumpet blowing.

The Bolchevicks also declared that there was no God, but if there was, he should move out of Russia, so hardly surprising that when they were going downhill they could not expect any blessings. Yes, perhaps we can live without blessings from God, but only barely. And that's how the Russian people had to live. Barely. Poor and without joy, and with grumbling stomachs and an ocean of tears.

At one point I was working alone at the woodworking shop. When I asked for a helper, the management assigned a man to me whose name was Franz Gauf. He was about forty years of age. Friendly, hardworking and honest, he came from Frankfurt. He had no children, but was happily married. He talked often about his life at home and had only good things to say about his wife.

When spring came we could use glue again. To make the glue we received a yellowish caseine powder. We mixed this with water and soda. This mixture turned almost transparent. Then it could be used. The Russians told us that the soaked powder, before the addition of soda, could be eaten. Thereafter we ordered and used up a lot of glue. Within two months I increased my weight by three kilos.

Chapter 12
Labour Camps

May, 1947

We volunteered to work on a Kolchos (State Farm). We thought that everyone who produces food also has food to eat. But that was not the case in the U.S.S.R.

We went on a thirty kilometer march to get there. When we were twelve kilometers from our goal we came to an area where the road was flooded by spring melt water from ice and snow. This was ten meters wide and reached up to our belt line. The Russian Sergeant rode through. We walked through, though the water was icy. Considering our starved condition and lack of sleep, it was more than we could take. Since early morning everybody suffered silently. We still had to walk some twelve kilometers in our wet shoes and wet clothes.

When we arrived at our destination we found only a small log hut about five meters square. Nothing else. There was no food for us. We lay down on the floor of the hut like sardines in a can and fell asleep in our wet clothes.

Somebody woke me up at five in the morning to build a fire under the soup kettle. The soup would have been ready to serve at seven AM except that the Russian decided that we should march to the village of Moskwa first to pick up three hundred kilograms of nails and tools. The cook protested, suggesting that we wait another thirty minutes to give the men a chance to have their soup and bread. It would have been their first food in twenty-four hours. However, the Sergeant didn't want to wait. He left with twenty men at 6:30 AM.

I didn't have to go because I was working as a kitchen helper. I had to get the fires burning. When I watched the twenty men with the Russian walk down to the forest, I knew that these men were on the brink of disaster. Finally they disappeared among the trees. These men now had to walk twenty-six kilometers and for half that distance they would each be weighted down under fifteen kilogram packs.

Seven hours later one man walked out of the forest. He had bad news. At least ten men were down on the muddy road with the nail bags strapped to their backs. Some of them were dying.

We were told to fill a barrel with soup, load it onto a two-wheel cart and the Sergeant's little horse would pull it. We found eight men on the road in a sad state, completely exhausted.

We fed some warm soup to one of the men. He swallowed it and smiled faintly. He did not talk. I thought that he knew that his suffering was over. He died soon after. Two more died a little later. We loaded some of the men onto the cart and brought our sad cargo back to the Kolchos.

Then we returned to pick up the rest.

During the rest of May we took down several abandoned log houses and assembled them on our kolchos.

June, 1947

The summer is short in west Siberia, so the time to sow a crop is June

when it grows very fast. There was only black soil available and it was five to ten meters deep. There were no stones to be found.

Toward the end of June the wild clover, more than 80 centimeters high, had to be cut. We were given the blade of a scythe, for which we had to make a handle from green wood in the forest. Five of us were assigned to cut a measured three thousand square meters of clover per day or we would not get any bread. There were hundreds of square kilometers of wild clover growing in the Taige, a land that also had forest and swamps. We built hay stack after hay stack. It was to be picked up in winter and sold on the black market by high ranking officers. They used American Studebaker trucks to bring it to the market. Those trucks were all paid for by U.S. tax payers.

We had to do this work, bare foot, during the summer. Our boots had been taken away mid-May and were given back to us on October first.

August, 1947

We packed saws, axes, and a pot for cooking on a small Siberian horse called Rischka. We also brought some rope along to pull the pine trees to the street. They needed

5 meter logs. These were not intended to build up the fatherland, but to be sold on the black market.

We marched west for ten kilometers. It was a hot day and there were dense clouds of mosquitoes. When we reached our destination we found no building of any kind. Because the night was not far, we dug holes and covered them with branches and earth. We used our only blanket to block the entrance to keep the stinging insects out. Then we had to build a small hearth in which to burn moss. It did not burn with a flame. It smoldered and produced smoke that drove out the mosquitoes.

We had with us our bread rations for one week. We found water for making our soup in a nearby brook. We were promised that we would soon receive rations for the following week. The week came to an end, with hard work and little food, but the new provisions did not come. We still had our instructions to cut so many meters of logs each day, but we had no food any more. What's more, all the cutting had to be done by hand because we had no machines or chainsaws.

I remember cutting trees with Gunter Kaiser from Bochum. He was a hard working, intelligent man. We stuffed rags under our caps to cover our necks against everything that stings. On the third day without food, Gunter stopped sawing and said, "Can you hear that? It sounds like a motor. They are coming with our food." But there was no motor. No food. The sound was simply the humming of a big bumble bee. All day Gunter heard motors. I was suffering, also, but my brain did not play tricks. Watching Gunter's desperation, however, caused me a lot of pain.

In the afternoon I walked one kilometer to the next village and collected stinging nettles, a plant that stings, but when cooked, is edible. I washed the dust away at the brook and boiled them so that at least we had something to eat.

While the nettles were still boiling, a Russian came along the road waving a birch branch around his head to keep the flies away. He saw me and came to my fire.

"Strastwiche," (Hello) he said. "Can I ask you what you are cooking?" "Yes," I told him. "It is stinging nettles and water." "Is it good?" he asked. "It is not what we want to eat," I answered, "but we hope that it keeps us alive." "Oh, it smells so good," he said. "Do you think I could get a bowl full when it is finished?" "Yes, you can have some," I said, "but tell me, where are you going?" He said he was walking to Velijano. "Well," he explained, "I am the school teacher in the village where the nettles grow. I am paid 4 kg. of bread every week, but I have to pick it up in Velijano."

Now, here was a school master, without shoes, hungry like a wolf, who had to walk forty kilometers to bring his bread home. The Russians had an expression: Organisazi blochoi (bad organization). The mismanagement in the Soviet Union was a stagnating cancer that killed not only the economy, but also the very lives of the people.

I gave him a bowl of "soup screpiwa." While he spooned it out he asked me if I ever got mail from home. "Yes" I said. "I received a very short letter not long ago." He wanted to know what my parents said in their letter. I said, " They have butter, meat, sugar and everything else they need."

"There you have it," he said. "We won the war and we have nothing, and you lost it and yet have all the food you want."

He thanked me for the soup, took up his birch branch and moved on.

The next day the Sergeant of the Kolchos came on horseback to deliver our bread and a few pounds of flour with which to colour our soup a bit so it could be more than just clear water. Because the mosquitoes during the night in the forest were more than anybody could endure, he led us to the village so we could sleep in the house of a widow.

The widow's husband had died on the Front Line. There was also her pretty young daughter, who did not talk to us because her fiancé had also died on the front. There were two young boys sitting on the pietschku, a walled up hearth resembling a bread baking oven of olden times. I believe that these boys were twins, about eight years of age. Both were mentally retarded and physically handicapped due to starvation. It was the saddest house I've ever seen. I suspect that there were many houses like this all over this deprived land. Only an ungodly society could treat a widow like this after she had given her husband for her motherland.

As soon as the Sergeant was out of the house, the widow complained in tears about the injustice and disrespect she received from the government. She also added that she wanted to die. We asked her if it was not possible to survive with the milk of her cow and some potatoes, but she explained that she had to deliver all the cream from the milk to the Bolshevik government agent.

It was nice being in a real house again. Here we could eat our food under a roof, morning and night. Every morning while we had our soup and bread a very old man with a long white beard came to the house. He went down on his knees and folded his hands together and begged for a little bread. He looked up at us with tears in his eyes. The widow helped him up, explaining that we had not enough bread to do the hard work in the forest. There was none to spare. The old man forced a smile while he was backing out, still bowing. An elderly woman also came to the house begging for bread, but, again, there was none to spare.

The pain in me was immense. I wanted to avenge the inhuman behavior of the merciless Soviets. But God said, "Don't do anything like that. The time will come when I will avenge, when I will ask them to pay for every soul they enslaved."

Several days later the Sergeant came to us to tell us that we could not sleep in the village any more. We had to go back to our holes again. I think that he was afraid that we might see and hear too much.

One day I felt very weak. Since I still had a five gram soap bar in one of my pockets, I walked back to the village and into the house of the widow. I gave her the tiny soap bar in exchange for a cup of skim milk.

While I was drinking the milk, the police officer walked in and asked the widow why her daughter did not report to work. She explained that her daughter had tuberculosis and could not walk. The officer started yelling. He pulled the sick girl from her bed and threw her into the street.

I stood there, horrified, not able to do anything. This same officer once held a cocked pistol to my head for no reason. He tortured people and animals alike. Many years later I prayed to God that his punishment not be too severe.

When I walked out of the widow's house into the street, a man called out to me. He was a former soldier and he had brought a bicycle all the way from Germany to Siberia, without an air pump. His rear tire was flat. He asked me to repair the damage. I asked him for the pump. He said "Nieto" (I have none). So I told him that I could not help him. He could not understand why a German could not repair a German bicycle. He was really disappointed in me.

We still had a few days of work to do before marching back to the Kolches. But when we finally arrived there, we were told that a group of women would take over to do our work. I had questions about these women who, obviously, would be treated like work horses. Where did they come from? Where were their husbands? Where were their children? Where was the hearth on which they could cook meals. I thanked God that my mother and my sister did not have to suffer in a place like this. And there were hundreds of thousands of such places. Was this the utopian society Lenin promised to build--without God?

We departed from Velijano and when the sun went down in the west, we arrived back at Camp 2.

Chapter 13
Potato Harvest

September, 1947

I have always thought September to be the best month of the year. The birches turn golden, and the geese fly south in formation, free!

We were not free. One day, after coming back to the barracks after work, I found Franz Gauf sitting all alone at the end of the yard. His head was down. He was motionless, staring at the ground. Something must be terribly wrong. Franz was never the depressed type.

I walked over to him. He did not look up. When I asked him what happened, he lifted his right hand, holding a letter toward me.

Three months ago we were given permission to write our first letters home. We were allowed to write only fifteen words, including the address. Now the first replies were arriving.

When I read the letter, I saw that it came from his sister. She explained that his letter reached his wife three months too late. Convinced that he was no longer alive, she had committed suicide.

The days dragged by ever so slowly. We lost all hope

of returning to our motherland. The war had ended two years ago. We could do nothing but wait.

Our officers were all held in Moscow, and fed very well, but we, the working class people of Germany, were slowly but surely dying of starvation. That was clearly in violation of the Bolshevik manifesto, which claimed that they, the Bolchevicks, were fighting for the "working class of all nations."

Three months later the ten weakest men were allowed to go home. Among them was Franz. I was so glad for him. Oh, how I wanted to be with him on this difficult but wonderful journey home.

The day came for the ten men to walk toward the gate, and freedom. We were all standing nearby to see these fortunate men walk out. Franz walked without lifting his head. It was the best he could manage. We went through such hard and hungry times together. We even shared the last morsel of food together. Still, all through these hard days we had hoped to go home together. To be able to say to each other: "We finally made it!" When Franz walked out through the gate, and it closed behind him, it was my turn to hang my head because I knew that I would never see him again.

A few days later we had to walk to yet another kolchos. It was the kolches near Cherwichov. We had to walk sixty kilometers without stopping, and without food.

On that excruciating march, the man beside me was a Bavarian, and still able to smile, even though his legs were not made for such an exercise. His name was Hans Huber. He was a good young man and when we finally arrived in Cherwichov we decided that we would work together. Many prisoners were loners, but I did not want to go it alone. In Siberia, a friend can be all you have.

Our new location had good log huts. There was also a new Banja (bathhouse) that had been constructed by an advance party.

Our first day of work had us put a new straw roof on an older barn. There were no animals on that kolches. They had most likely been eaten long ago, around the time of the revolution in 1917.

Because there was no straw, we walked down into a swamp, a kilometer away, to cut bulrushes that were growing in abundance to a height of eight feet. The bundles of bulrushes were so huge that the men carrying them were scarcely visible.

On the way back we had to walk uphill, toward the kolchos. Since we were still exhausted from the twenty-hour march, and because our sweating provided a field day for the stinging beasts, we were a sorry lot indeed.

For the next two weeks we made hay. Then the potatoes had to be harvested. The potato field was huge, and of course there were no machines to help with the harvest.

When we first arrived at the field in the morning, we asked the Russian in charge to give us the tools for digging out the potatoes. He shook his head and said to wait until we got to where we were to start work. He came with us, and when we did get there he walked to the edge of the forest, broke off a branch the thickness of a finger, pushed it into the ground and said: "Here you have it, that's the way you have to do it."

We worked all of September on that potato field. Hans and I carried potatoes up to the camp. The transport was done with bushel baskets. A sapling was pushed through both handles, lifted up to our shoulders, and we carried that load uphill for two hundred meters to the potato bunker.

We started the job at seven every morning and ended our days at sundown. Throughout all those days we watched the geese in their freedom, high above us streaming southward.

It was a beautiful area, but hard. Perhaps someone with good will and health could have made a good living off the land here. It was virgin soil, and fertile. But to make a success of it, the people would have to be free. Free to sell their produce in town.

Instead, slaves produced the food, which was sold on the black market. Because the government couldn't pay sufficient wages to the army and government officials, they were given a free hand to operate in whatever way would be profitable to them. That was unjust to the population, of course. Especially to the working class. They could not afford to pay black market prices to buy back their own produce! But the army and the officials were the pillars of the Soviet system. The working man and the old widows were not important. Nor were the children.

And so we continued carrying potatoes up the hill to the bunker all day long, bare foot. But there was a good side to it. Hans and I had time to talk about our lives at home. We also talked about our future. At least we still had hope that we had a future.

One day there was a cold rain. The earth turned into a soupy mud. Soon the rain had soaked our clothes and was trickling down our bodies. We fell silent because we needed all our energy to work to the end of the day. We came back to an unheated camp and, because our clothes were also our pyjamas, we had to go to sleep as wet as we were. We were often still wet in the morning. Oh, how appreciative we were of the sun, rising up over the forest. How wonderful it was to feel the warm rays on our dark clothes. Such moments of great joy this simple pleasure gave us.

In order to give us strength to do this field work of digging potatoes, we ate a lot of raw potatoes. Of course we had to eat them without being discovered. We didn't dare to stuff them into a fire to roast them. If they had caught us doing that they would have transferred us into a penal unit, where the men had to work in chains.

Toward the end of September, the geese were still honking high above. We had the feeling that we, alone, were left to face the grim winter months.

One evening the uniformed manager called us all out. He led us to the road to Cherwichov. After we had walked two kilometers, we turned to the left and uphill, right to the edge of the forest. We were then on the grounds of a private kolchos. Stalin allowed them to operate without government supervision in order to find out how profitable they would be.

There was a plate-tiller standing there. We dismantled it under orders of the manager, and carried it completely away. There were hardly any tracks visible, because the earth was frozen solid.

During the following week we had to cut several tree trunks into boards. The tree was placed on top of two scaffolds. A man on top had to pull a huge saw blade up and a man underneath pulled down. It was very hard work and we could cut only four boards per day.

November, 1947

It was cold, and there was snow. We had to work in the potato bunker to sort the rotten potatoes out. We were locked in this bunker with several oil lamps. When our eyes got used to the dark, we could see five air shafts going up through the roof. Each had two shutters, one inside the bunker and one on the top, above the roof. I had to find a way to get some of these potatoes out through the air shafts.

We were in a deadly situation. Without nourishment we would succumb to starvation, tuberculosis and eventual death. We had a choice. We could resign ourselves to death, or take the risk and fight for survival. I decided to find a way to get some of those potatoes.

In the evening I walked all over the kolchos, hoping to find inspiration. I found a length of wire and a heavy screw nut. When it was dark enough I walked up the back side of the bunker roof, opened the shutter and dropped the screw nut attached to the wire down the shaft. I could hear the nut hitting the closed shutter on the bottom of the shaft. I closed the top shutter and attached the wire to the shutter handle.

In the morning, the guard locked us in again. Hans looked through a split in the door to see if anybody approached the bunker from the direction of the camp. When the coast was clear I opened the shutter and the nut fell to the floor. I loosened the nut from the wire and pierced the wire through twenty good sized potatoes. Then I attached the screw nut on the end of the wire, stuffed the bundle up into the air shaft, and closed the shutter on the bottom.

That evening I climbed up to the shaft, took the nut in one hand, opened the shutter with the other, and pulled the twenty potatoes up. Then I tied the circuit of potatoes around my waist, put my coat on over it, and walked down to the bath-house.

The advance party who had built the bath-house did a good job of it. The walls were made of logs. Two of these logs could be removed. There was a space behind the removable logs to hide potatoes or anything that could be stolen to be eaten in safety later.

There was a big hearth built with two barrels to heat water for our body wash. Between the water barrels was a 30 centimeter square, covered by a sheet of steel. The steel panel could be removed only with a hook made from a piece of wire. We could then lower a cooking pot into the extension of the burning chamber. The steam of the cooking food moved out the chimney with the smoke of the fire.

Nobody wanted to lift the metal sheet because it was very hot. Walter Gimbach was the bath master and also the engineer of this life-giving arrangement. He had a small window built in facing the kolchos. We had to guard not only against the Russians, but also against the German managers--who were much more dangerous.

When I showed up at Walter's place that evening, I opened my coat to display my "potato belt." He was surprised and delighted at the same time. The logs were removed and the potatoes stored.

Over the next few days Walter cooked several pots of potatoes. We had a few good moments in the bath-house, with either Hans Huber or myself on look-out so that no harm could come to us.

A short time later I was sent to Cherwichov to bring a message to one of our men who worked there. On the way home, while still in the village, I saw a little girl dressed in the German style. I asked her if she spoke German. She said, "Yes, my mama, too. Do you want to speak with her?" I said that I would be delighted to speak with her. The little girl walked with me to a nearby house. The door opened and there was her mama, a friendly person with a smile that seemed to be hiding sadness.

She invited me in. We were sitting on wooden benches in her one room house, which was more than humble. She told me that she was a teacher, as was her husband, who was Russian. She was born in a Volga German village, and shipped to Siberia with the entire population of her village. Stalin did not trust them.

She told me over and over again that I was lucky because sooner or later I would go home, but she could never go home because her village was given over to Russians. I parted, saying that I wished her and her family good health and the blessings of God and that one day she would go home to her village on the shores of the Volga River, where she was born.

On my way home, I found a Tartar man lying in the muddy road. He must have been on his way to our kolchos to find some potatoes that had been overlooked. Here he was, dying. He was not an old man, but very frail. I wanted to pull him to dry ground, but he motioned to me to let him be. It took all his energy to tell me to go away. So I left. But the pain in my heart was enormous.

The Tartars were all Muslims, living on the Crimea. They were the left overs from Tchingdiscan. Stalin shipped them all to Siberia. He refused to deal with them, or employ them. They were made beggars in a harsh land where everybody was hungry.

A kolchos eight kilometers away needed help fast. Several workers there were ill and a hay stack had to be brought under a roof before the first snow fell. With four men and an old Russian guard, we set out early in the morning. The old man carried a twelve gauge shotgun.

After arriving there we started our job of moving the hay. We did it the Siberian way. We forked a good pile together, pushed two saplings underneath, lifted it all up and walked through the gate of the hay barn. When we had a short break I looked around in that barn and found a pile of potatoes in a corner, covered with straw. I also found a tin pail. I counted twenty potatoes into the pail, walked over a hill, and made a fire with old boards and branches. I covered the opening of the pail with grass, turned the pail around, with the opening toward the ground, and built the fire around it. After two hours I pulled the pail around and all the potatoes were cooked. We were four men, plus the old man. Each received four big potatoes. The guard did not understand. He asked me if those four potatoes were for him. I told him, yes. He looked at me, his eyes filling with tears. He mumbled that he had not seen so much food in a long time.

When I looked at that frail old man, I saw all the suffering of the Russian people personified in front of me.

The first snow fell, but several days later it melted away. This was unusual for that part of the world.

There was still a lot of work to be done in and around another huge potato bunker four kilometers to the east of the kolchos. The bunker was filled, but there was still a pile of one hundred tons at a location near Cherwichov. The Tartar walked with us to that pile. It started snowing while we were on our way. It was a wet snow. We were still wearing summer clothes.

Upon our arrival we could see the results of Soviet agriculture. They were like five-year olds who don't realize that winter is coming or that these potatoes will eventually freeze if not stored properly. Our little Tartar told us to pull grass out and cover the pile of potatoes to prevent it from freezing. There were hungry people around, like us, at the kolchos. Like the entire population of Cherwichov. Better to feed the living hungry than lose the harvest.

Now should have been the time to act for the good of the people, but no, they wanted to save face so now, in the middle of a wet snow storm, we had to pull snowed-over grass out with our bare hands to try to save the situation.

Icy water ran down our bodies as we worked. The Tartar took cover behind the only tree in that field. His black, mongoloid eyes showing no emotion. We were so cold and wet there was no hope of finishing the job. After two hours, even the Tartar had had enough. He called us together and led us to a cow barn at the edge of the village. For the Tartar this might have been just another cow barn, but for us it was a cow barn from hell. There were cows in that barn. The flat tin roof was very old and badly rusted. Streams of water splashed down into pools, mixed with cow manure. There were some shallow islands in those puddles, We were standing on one of the islands. The Tartar looked at me, with a sheepish smile.

The whole thing made no sense at all. If only they could throw their guns away and let people grow their own food. As it was, the crop had grown, it had ripened, the potatoes were harvested, but because there was no logic and no dialogue with the people the potatoes froze and the land was hungry.

During the last month four of our men dug out a three meter deep hole near the bunker. They built a roof over it. A stairway was installed and a door hung. Now we had underground quarters that would house six men who would work all winter in and around the bunker.

Because there was more work to do on the shelter, we could not return to the kolchos that evening and because the earth shelter was neither finished, nor enclosed, we slept in the bunker on piles of moist potatoes, in our wet clothing. Before I fell asleep I munched on two raw potatoes. My body needed something to burn. When the earth shelter was finished we moved back to the kolchos. Hans had been worried about us, and bid me a friendly welcome.

Chapter 14
Garlic

November, 1947

For the next two weeks, Emil, Hans and I cut firewood not far from the camp. Now the land was frozen hard. Each morning, after arriving at the birch forest, we built a good fire. There were no matches, so we carried a primitive device with us that could produce a flame. It was a thirteen centimeter steel pipe with a diameter of one and a half centimeters, with a round wick inside. The wick hung down on the bottom part of the pipe and just protruded at the top end of the pipe. Striking downward toward the protruding wick with a blue pebble produced a spark against the wick. Soon a tiny bit of smoke appeared and, with a gentle blowing against the wick a sustained glow was produced. All that was needed then was a bit of birch bark and a few tiny dry branches and the fire could be started.

November, 1947

We were loading hay from outlying wild clover patches

onto Studebaker trucks destined for the black market in Tyumen.

One day I went to bring a message to the group at the earth shelter. It was a bitterly cold day, but thankfully we now had good sheepskin clothing and high felt boots. It was an odd feeling to walk all alone in this land of Siberia, over fields and through forests. I recall that it was the first time I was alone in this harsh land, that I was able to feel a deep peace in my heart.

When I arrived there at noon, the whole gang of six were sitting around a table. The inside of the earth shelter was now very comfortable. These men were very friendly toward me and, because I was their visitor, they sang some wonderful songs from our homeland. I was able to fall in with the second accord. We sang for about thirty minutes and somehow, with the singing, the bitterness moved from our hearts.

Karl, the foreman, asked me to stay with them, but, because that was not possible, he had another idea. He said, "Go back and talk to the Tartar and tell him that we need you here because of your potato conservation experience."

So I left, promising to do my best. It was a very cold afternoon. My eye lids were heavy with hoar frost. When I arrived at the camp the German veterinarian (in the rank of a general), was there. Nobody needed him, really, because we had only one pig. He looked at me and smiled and said: "Scherer, you look almost like a film diva."

I found the Tartar, and after I gave him Karl's message he agreed that I should move to the bunker the next morning.

I said good-bye to Hans the next morning, promising to come back as soon as possible.

The one aspect of moving to the earth shelter that determined my decision was the freedom that I could have there. There were no Russian or German pushers there. Most of us were willing to do our obligations, but we did not like the arrogance and the trickery, particularly of the German officials. They were opportunists of the worst kind.

I walked slowly toward the earth bunker. Not because I had to carry such heavy a load. No, indeed I carried nothing at all. I owned nothing. Not even a handkerchief. All my pockets were empty. All I had was the clothes on my body. The reason I walked so slowly was because I wanted to savour my freedom and my aloneness as long as possible. I felt again like a free man on God's earth. The strength that I felt did not come out of my starved body, nor from my tormented brain. It came to me from my everlasting helper, who had saved my life so many times before. It was Him who walked with me. And it was not in the mild air of my motherland, but in the unforgiving cold of this land of Siberia.

Arriving at the shelter, I walked down the stairs. When I pushed the door it opened with a screech and a cloud of warm air turned into white fog and rushed up the staircase.

While I sat at the table with Karl, talking about materials we still needed, a burning oil drum stove made it all so cozy. But we still needed boards to cover the walls and also the staircase walls.

A few days later, the Tartar showed up. When we asked him for boards he walked with us one kilometer to the north, where we found a railway car standing without wheels. The Tartar said that after our assigned job was done we could salvage those boards left from the railway car walls.

That railway car was not there by accident. It had been pulled there by tractor operators who lived in it while plowing and seeding great tracts of land. When they came back in spring to do the plowing, we were gone. And so were the boards from the railway car walls.

After work the next morning we removed all the boards from the railway car and carried them to our place. It took us two days to carry that wall away. With two men we covered the walls and staircase in eight days.

Now we were to concentrate on sorting out the rotten potatoes. We started right next to the door and worked our way toward the far end of the bunker.

We always sat two men on a pile. The foul potatoes were thrown into a basket and the good ones behind us. The two men had one oil lamp, which was really only an American tin can with a piece of a rag as a wick. This lamp smoked so badly that our faces were black after eight hours.

We always worked with the same man. My partner was a man from Nuremberg. His name was Gustel. He told me his entire life story from when his mother placed him in a bundle in front of a Protestant pastor's door, to his life on the Front Line, where he destroyed seven T-34 Russian tanks in one day with hand-held rockets. He always wore the certain smile of a man who could not be conquered. Fear played no part in his life.

Some days it was so warm inside and so cold outside that when we stepped outside we steamed like hot potatoes in winter.

One of our men complained about diarrhea. His condition worsened and, a week later he died. We buried him not far from the shelter. Two weeks later a second man had the same illness. He fought it for three weeks. He was then transferred by horse and sleigh to the kolchos. They had no medication to fight the virus. He also died and was buried there. After three weeks I got the same sickness. I had a sinking feeling. I knew that I had only one to three weeks to fight it. But all I could do now was continue with my work. Oh, we sang still, every evening. I think the men did not realize the extent of the virus infection in my bowels. We had no toilet inside and only a ditch a few yards from our stairs as a latrine. To get up and out to that ditch was a heroic act.

On the third day of my virus infection, I suddenly had a strong craving for garlic. I hardly knew garlic because my mother never used it, but still the craving grew stronger by the hour. One of our men had to go to Cherwichov to get our bread ration for several days. Since I was a non-smoker, I had a pouch of tobacco to trade with. I told the man to bring me as much garlic as possible.

I went back to the bunker with Gustel, but I could hardly wait for the man to return from Cherwichov with the garlic. When our work day was done he returned from the village with bread, and with five bulbs of garlic. I cleaned one of the bulbs immediately, cut it in pieces with my home made knife, and dumped it into my soup. The aroma was heavenly. I spooned it down and enjoyed every spoon full. Right there and then I had a wonderful feeling of well-being. I knew that the virus was beaten.

When I lay down on my bunk that evening I thanked God, who had saved me one more time. Garlic was the only medication that could save me and was available for miles around.

Chapter 15
Good News

December 1947

It was so cold that Karl was afraid we would lose all the potatoes. He suggested adding some earth to the roof of the potato bunker. Because the earth outside was frozen hard, we removed the boards from the lower bunk beds and started digging there. We loaded the loose earth from under the bunk bed into baskets and dumped it on the snow covered roof of the potato bunker. The hole under the bunk bed grew deeper and deeper. By morning there was fifty centimeters of water in it.

When we finished with the roof I made a box, lowered it into the hole, packed earth around it, and now we had a supply of water in our shelter even on the coldest day.

Toward Christmas the temperature rose and we felt, for a few, brief days, that spring was not so far away. But, of course, we knew that winter lasts until at least April in Siberia.

24 December, 1947

One morning Karl said: "Boys, today is Christmas Eve. We do not have to work both days, so what will we do to get ready for this evening. We all committed ourselves to doing the jobs that had to be done before evening. I took over the firewood splitting. Fritz Froehlich decided he should find a Christmas tree. While I was swinging the axe, Fritz came by and asked me where he should go for a tree. I turned to the east and pointed to the horizon. There was a dark spot within a birch forest. It could only be a growth of pine. Fritz gave me a tired smile and started walking. His goal was about five kilometers away.

I have recalled this moment many times over the years, and I always see the tired undernourished figure of Fritz walking toward the morning light.

It was nearly dark when he returned with a beautiful, one meter high tree over his shoulder. He had had no food all day. He did not complain, but he was exhausted.

Karl nailed the tree to the table top. We pulled thread out of a rag, then we rolled one end into a paper ball and so decorated the tree.

In the evening we had a generous portion of mashed potato plus soup and bread. We carried the big table, with the tree and all, into a new addition to our shelter. It was niche that was elevated by two steps. We all sat around the table and sang many old Christmas songs.

That evening was the high point in our existence as prisoners of war in Russia.

We had two good days, but they passed by quickly.

January, 1948
Thank God for men like Gustel, Franz, Gauf, Huber, Hans and Walter Gimbach. I found consolation just being

around them. Their personalities were varied, but they were all great friends.

Then one day the Russian manager arrived from the kolchos to tell us that we had to produce dried potatoes. To do so, we had to build a hearth, and install two barrels horizontally. We also needed grills inside the barrels to dry the potato slices on. We told the Russian that we would start to work on it as soon as we could get the materials.

"No," he said, "you have to get it yourself." He told us to walk to Cherwichov where we would find a fenced in oil storage area. He said that there was an old woman with a shot gun as a guard. But, he assured us that she was asleep most of the time.

"The guardhouse is on the west side, so you climb the fence on the east side." he said. "It's all very easy."

We were told to do all this in the dark. He provided a sled on which to bring the barrels home. The grills would have to be taken out of brand new thrashing machines, which we found outside the village. The Tartar led us to an abandoned house in the village, where we found the bricks needed for the hearth.

Within four days we were all set to operate. Karl organized day and night shifts to dry as many potatoes as possible, all for the black market in Tyumen.

The land was cannibalized to extend the power of the Bolsheviks, but as a result the Russian people had to do with less.

April 1948
When Russian prisoners took over the kolchos we

had to go back to Camp 2. Arriving at the camp, we were summoned for examination. Again we had to stand naked in front of a female medical doctor. She had a list in her hand and called one after another to be grouped into a certain category. Those men grouped in category one had to do heavy work, but category three could hope to go home.

I was grouped in category one again, and Hans was category three.

A new list of those men who would go home was soon posted. My friend Hans Huber was on the list. It was now April, 1948. The war had ended in May, 1945.

A few days later the group designated to go home assembled. All the prisoners to remain were there to see them off. The door opened and the fortunate men walked out for the last time.

Hans saw me and gave me his last smile. It was also the last time I ever saw him. I was happy for Hans but, after the door shut sadness overcame me. There are no words to describe my feelings.

May, 1948

At the end of May I had to go once again to Velijano. We were twenty men. We hated to go to that place, especially with that German manager, Statzner, whom everybody dreaded. We had seen too many men die there.

The sowing was all done, but it was too early to cut clover. There was really nothing better to do than cutting lumber.

Then Statzner had a diabolical idea. He marched us to

the swamp and told us to cut only trees that were standing in the water. May is not a balmy month in Siberia. The snow had only melted two weeks earlier and there was still ice just below the water's surface.

We waded in. The icy water reached above our knees. We were barefoot and standing on the slippery ice. The situation was fierce. We worked with the Swedish saws that had to be pulled from each end. I was cutting with Gunther Kaiser. Emil Schmit and Kurt Weise were cutting twenty meters from us. We were cutting our second tree when we heard a loud splash. We called out to inquire if all was right. Then I heard Kurt Weise call for help. As I approached them I could see Emil in the water. Kurt held his head up. Emil was unconscious. We pulled him to dry land and revived him. We had to carry him one kilometer back to the kolchos. He'd had a heart attack,

That evening, while we stood in line to be counted, Kurt Weise fell forward, hitting the ground hard. He also had a heart attack.

The Russian Sergeant stopped the cutting of trees in the swamp.

June 1948

During the whole month of June we cut clover and grass. We made hay and put it up into stacks. It was a hard, but peaceful work. I would have liked it if I could have done it in the free world, with some food and without the fear of dying young because of malnutrition and neglect.

For one day I had to assist a farmer who was plowing a huge field. A Russian officer approached. We greeted each other and, because it was a very hot and humid day, he asked me for water. But, of course, we did not have any. Then he asked for a cup, but there was no cup, either. He then took a diesel pail, pushed it into a black puddle of water, swirled it around, emptied it and pushed the pail back into the puddle. Then he lifted the pail to his mouth and drank. I was speechless. I doubted that I could live with conditions where he could still survive.

On another occasion I had the same feeling of inferiority. We were helping out at another kolchos. When our work was done we were led to a kitchen barracks where we were given a bowl of watery soup. The two young women behind the counter spoke a German dialect. They were Volga Germans. When we approached them, they told us that they admired our good manners. I laughed and said that we were as hungry as wolves and also ate like them. While I was talking with the younger woman, two Tartar women walked in.

They seemed to me to have a wild look about them with their brown faces and mongolic features. When they saw us, they started to giggle. They received soup and a handful of small, salted fishes with heads on, complete with scales and intestines. They ate outside, sitting on a log. It was just a few degrees above freezing. They crunched the little fish with their snow white teeth and laughed and giggled. Once again I had the feeling that I would die, whereas they could still thrive.

July, 1948
Eight of us had to go to yet another Kolchos to help out.

The place we went to was much more civilized than what we had seen before. There were villages, fields, wooded hills and a deep, clear brook. We were needed to transport flax from fields into a hay barn.

We had no housing there. We lived under a pine tree, beside a brook. I cooked for all of us, but there was really nothing to cook with. The soup came out of the brook. A handful of flour and a spoon and salt was all we had to put in, plus some birch mushrooms that we could find almost everywhere.

It was hot and the brook was deep enough to swim in and since we did not have a Russian guard with us, we felt very good. I could go for a swim several times a day, Swim wear was unknown in Siberia at this time.

One day, toward evening, I enjoyed the cool water one more time when I heard a woman singing a German song in a loud voice, high up on the wooded hill, opposite our camp.

I called up, "Wonderful, wonderful!!! and what a nice song. come down and say 'hello' to us."

She came down and greeted us with a warm smile. I asked her why she was singing all the way up the mountain. She told us that she was singing because she was a little afraid to go home all alone in the forest. She was an unspoiled seventeen year old. The daughter of Volga German parents. She also had to help at another kolchos.

Although I was standing deep enough in the water, I apologized for not having any swim wear, but she laughed and said that I should not worry because nobody had special clothes for bathing. She told me that in her village the children swam during the day up to three PM, then it was the young men's turn. Then came the young women, and toward evening the older people come to the brook to bathe. She assured me that there was never a problem.

I thought, thank God there is a place on earth without a problem. A deep brook, a wooded mountain and a lot of mushrooms. Maybe, after all, there might be a place in Siberia where I, too, could live.

The years in Siberia seemed like an eternity. My hopes of going home faded slowly away since the police officers knew about my opposition to the Bolsheviks. Maybe I could live in one of the villages nearby, beside the brook. I knew that, despite everything, I would never forget God, who, in his unending love, had saved my life so many times. Maybe he could save me one more time and give me a chance to live in a place like this village on a brook, and maybe have a dear wife and a child and make my life a success, at least in His eyes.

August, 1948

Our job beside the brook came to an end. We returned to Velijano with a heavy heart. The next day the Sergeant walked with us to a barley field of twenty acres. With sickles in our hands we cut and tied the bundles.

A few days later the Sergeant came out with us to build an enormous stack. Because it was a damp day we suggested that we should wait for a dry day to do the job. The Sergeant smiled at us and told us to start.

Three weeks later we came back to the field. We could see that the stack was overheated inside. The barley was fermenting and spoiled. While we were there we searched and collected barley grains that were still on the ground for our own use. Another example of uniformed people with no training making wrong decisions. And the Russian people suffered.

A few days later I was given five men and one old shovel and told to repair a swampy fifty meter stretch on the road to Velijano. The Sergeant rode along that road every day and several times his horse got stuck in the swamp.

Now, with our workforce, plus the one shovel, we had to fill that swamp with earth to make it a part of the road. Statzner gave me the responsibility, knowing full well that it was impossible to repair the road that way.

When the Sergeant came down the road from Velijano he complained that the road was still not repaired. Statzner called me out in front of all the men. He called me a "pus-boil on the body of mankind." Of course, he didn't impress me, or anybody else, but he condemned me to cut firewood for five nights until three AM. I then had to get up at five AM to fetch water from a well to the kitchen,

I did all this with a man named Stanislaus from Upper Celesia.

Nobody, not even Statzner could aggravate this man, or hurry him on. Therefore he was on permanent wood cutting duties. With two hours sleep we were certainly not the working heroes the next day and Statzner had a good excuse to extend our wood cutting sessions.

Before I came to Siberia I did not know that there were men among us who would push their brothers into a grave in order to save themselves. However, I suspect that these types can be found in every nation.

September, 1948

Toward the end of September, some of our men were still busy with the potato harvest. We had to go back to produce hay, also. It didn't much matter to them what the nutrition value of the dried up grass was. We left early in the morning to reach the wild meadows. There was a potato field in our path. We took some potatoes with us to cook in the forest. After we had cut our quota, we sat down in the forest to eat some of the cooked roots. It was, in a sense, a heroic act, because if they had found out, we could have been convicted and received another five years of forced labour.

Eventually our kidneys became so weak that we retained water. Our legs were badly swollen. One day, examining my legs, I wasn't sure I could survive another year. I was twenty-four years of age and it was September, 1948. The war had ended in May, 1945. Did nobody miss us? Did our motherland write us off? Our situation was desperate.

Suddenly, one morning in October, we were called out into the yard. The sergeant was there to tell us that we would march back to Tyumen that same morning, to be sent home to our motherland. We could hardly believe it. We received tooth brushes and tried to get our teeth white by brushing with wood ashes. We forgot that we were hungry. In the depths of our hearts we thought that the news was too good to be true.

Two hours later we were on our way. Some had small

bundles to carry. I had a piece of a dirty towel to bring along. It was my only precious possession.

After an hour of marching, it started raining. It was a cold rain, mixed with snow. We walked along a dirt road and into a forest and down into a gorge.

Chapter 16
Chosen

There were five trucks stuck on the lowest level of the gully. The truck drivers had a good fire going. They could not proceed further because the rain on black muck didn't allow them to climb up the hills. The land around Tyumen had no sand or stone, only three meters of black muck. The drivers never go anywhere without dried bread and water. They sat around the fire, waiting for dry weather.

They asked us where we were going. When we answered, "Back home to Germany," they said, "Never! You are going to Verchojansk, which is the worst town in northern Siberia." They certainly did not wish us well.

I walked with miserable Russian shoes, and barefoot. Toward evening we saw the lights of Tyumen. I sat down and examined my feet. I found open, bleeding wounds. I got up fast and walked along barefoot on frozen ground right to the door of Camp 2 in Tyumen.

When we called out to the guard, he told us that we had to wait for all the men to arrive. So we sat down and rested.

I looked to the west, where there was still some light left. It also gave me time to say goodbye to Velijano. I loved the land around it. Nature was always good to me and I loved it dearly. Despite the hunger and poverty, I had met some good men there. They were often all that kept me sane in desperate times. It is hard to understand that even a place like this can mean a lot to a man who has to eat his poor portion of bread there, and lay his tired body to rest. I knew where I slept in Velijano, but where I was going, where would I sleep?

We had to wait one hour for the last men to arrive. We had made that long, cold journey without food or water. Now we would have to wait for morning to get our soup and bread.

Four years ago there were one thousand men in Camp 2. Now there were only three hundred of us left to go home. Most had died, and some were shipped home very sick, or very weak.

We sat on our bunks that evening, talking and dreaming about things to come.

In the morning I remembered a song I once heard. It was one of the songs of Lola Andersen. The text tells of a bouquet of poppies that were given to a girl. I sang that song over and over until a man in a dark corner of the barracks called me over. He was an engineer from East Germany. A very intelligent and good willed man, who had invented many things at the Velijano kolchos. He motioned to me to come nearer. He told me that the Russians had found out that he was a member of an organization in the third Reich (Hitler's party). He told me that he was not on the list of men who would go home. I was not aware that I, too, was not on that list. I tried to talk him out of his depression, but he would not even lift his head.

The night passed quickly and the next afternoon we were called out to the gate. The feeling of expectation, mixed with anxiety, was overwhelming. A nurse sat at a small table with the list of men who would soon walk out the door to go home. I wished that my name would start with "A" but it starts with Sch....

When the "s's" had passed and the names starting with "T" were called I was very worried. What I also did not know was that, in the Russian alphabet, the "Sch" comes after "Z." But when the "Z's" were at an end, there was only one more name on the list and it was the name "Schafer." But Schafer had gone home six months before. Now we were only two men inside the camp. Besides me, there was a Romanian named Oizen. He complained to the police officer that his name was not on the list, but the Russians had information that Oizen had been a tough Sergeant Major on the Front Line.

The officer waited Oizen out, but then he turned to him and slammed his hand right and left into Oizen's face. He told him to sit down on a bench. The Russian barber was called out to cut Oizen's hair off. The officer turned toward him and told him that his five years of hard labour would start right now. Up to now Oizen was one of the managers in the camp.

I talked with the nurse and convinced her that my name had been misspelled. It was not Schafer, but Scherer. She crossed Schafer out and replaced it with my name. The police commissar, Korodezki, stared at me. Perhaps my name had been left out to scare me.

No words can describe the joy and exaltation that

streamed through my whole being at that moment as I walked out of the gate. My friends were waiting for me. Their faces showed their concern that I might not be included, but when I walked out they all smiled. They knew that I was no friend of the Bolsheviks nor of the cruel German management. When I walked toward them, all I could say was, "We are going home now."

A police officer showed up at the gate and said, in perfect German, "You can go home now and we don't care what you think about us." With that he turned and walked away. It took only a minute longer for the guard to give the signal to march.

I lost many friends on the front lines, and even more in the awful death camps of Siberia. I can still visualize the defeated expression on their faces when they realized their final battle was lost. They were still young men, but there was not even enough life force left in them to allow them to go home to die.

The day was cold, but the sun was shining. We were as hungry as we had been all through the years, but now we didn't feel it.

While we walked along the Dura River, the stress and anxiety of that last hour lifted out of us. The men smiled and talked. Some had their arms across the shoulders of their good friends.

Then we crossed the bridge over the Dura River for the last time.

Chapter 17
Anticipation of Home

October, 1948

I looked over to the left at the mill on the high banks of the river. I had worked so many days and nights there, mostly during the bitterly cold winter months. I still remember pigeons and sparrows sitting in the freezing cold all winter on the electric wire. What a harsh land it is.

We walked through the joyless streets of Tyumen right to the train station. The train was waiting for us. It was now the end of October. There were ten cattle cars, filled with thick layers of straw. We divided into ten groups and entered the train. We did not bring anything to Siberia and now, we had nothing to bring westward, only our lives. But that was a lot, because millions came here, never to see home again. There was no heat in the cars, it's true, but nobody complained. We were going home.

The youngest of us was about twenty-four years old and the oldest, over forty. None of us were healthy. Our years in Siberia melted away, and we thought of our families as we had left them. What awaited us proved that time changes things. Some would find themselves visiting the graves of their entire families. Others would find out that their wives had remarried, thinking their husbands dead.

Many were going home only to die. But the younger men were still full of hope, and I was among them.

Suddenly the train moved with a jolt. We all shouted with joy because this time our voyage was westward.

We were now on the Trans-Siberian Railway, which had only one track. We often had to park on a turn-out track to wait for eastbound trains to pass.

A Russian Corporal, who had served at the gate in Tyumen, was with us as an escort. While the train was halted, we met him outside. He begged us to let him know well in advance before we rolled into Moscow, because he had to clean his shoes. He thought that Moscow was something like a Bolshevik heaven. But we were not there by a long shot. We climbed up the eastern slope of the Ural Mountains and descended down into the European part of Russia. Days later we arrived in Kazan. And several more days found us not far from Gorki.

We had plenty of time to look at this land, Russia. We saw that there had been no improvement since the end of the war. The villages and towns were rundown places showing no glimmer of hope. More depressing than that were the forced labour camps all along the rail line, with high fences and watchtowers on every corner. We talked about it and came to the conclusion that one third of the Russian population had either been shipped to Siberia or to a forced labour camp. Most of them would have been better off dead than to labour without adequate food, with families separated, each member going to an early end, all alone.

At the next stop the train took on water and wood.

We informed the Corporal that Moscow was only a few hundred kilometers down the track. He pulled on his uniform jacket, that had seen better days. He opened the grease box on one of the wagon wheels and massaged his boots with his bare hands. Now he was ready for the Mecca of the Communist world.

After we passed Moscow, he expressed disappointment because all he saw was a poor town and only log cabins. But of course the rails do not run over Red Square and along the Kremlin walls.

The train stopped often. Sometimes for several hours and sometimes for the whole night. In Breslitowsk, near the Polish border, we had to get off the train to be searched for the last time. We had to take our shirts off and lift our arms up. They examined our armpits for a number that all members of the S.S. organization had tattooed there. When the examining guard looked under my arms he came suddenly much nearer. I thought, if he looks any longer he will discover a number there, even if there is none. But the guard then went on to the man beside me. The little bit of blood left in my ravaged body was boiling. I never forgot this critical moment. If somebody with a number was found, he had to go to several more years of slave labour camps, or to his grave.

In Warsaw, young boys came to the train to sell wonderful loaves of bread, but we did not have a single ruble to buy any. The Russian guards kicked the boys from the train station. They, the guards, were angered to see that other nations had bread for sale, which was not the case in Russia.

Between Warsaw and the Polish border, I had a vision. God said, "Go home now, and stay there for a few years, and then go on to Canada." But I protested, saying that I didn't know Canada. I knew that it was the northern part of North America, but could I love it there? Was it not a land covered with ice and snow, like Siberia? Could I find a spruce tree there? Or a wild flower? Could I find a good young woman there, with whom to share my life? God did not have an answer to my questions.

November, 1948

After four weeks on the train we reached Frankfurt on the Oder, a frontier town between East and West Germany. There we received a soup that must have been cooked from a Russian recipe. It was something terrible.

A government official came, and told us to stand in line to receive thirteen Eastern Marks each. I asked him what we could buy with it. He told us that we could buy Communist Literature or a shot of brandy. I told him that we now knew what to buy. He asked me what it was.

When I told him that it was certainly Communist literature a hundred men standing around me roared with laughter. The Communist official smiled sheepishly and left.

Before we received the thirteen Eastern Marks, we had been sitting on bunks in a cold and damp barracks. It was then the end of November. Almost nobody spoke. We were hungry, tired and sick and concerned about what was waiting for us at home. After we received a small quantity of brandy, the cold barracks warmed up and everybody talked. It was as if the whole Soviet nightmare had gone back to Russia where it belonged. Early in the morning we were still on the train. We reached Leipzig by midday. And another day later we entered the American Zone. An American officer debriefed us, all in fluent German.

It was about supper time when we were led into a mess tent. We found long tables covered with white table cloths. The place was nicely illuminated. The tables were set with plates, forks, knives and spoons. We had not seen such niceties in more than four years.

Everybody had a full plate of milk noodles, coffee, bread, small portions of butter, sausage, cheese and marmalade. We hadn't expected that. We sat down and looked at all of that food. The pain in my chest was too much. While I was looking down tears fell freely. Yes, there was still human decency.

There are no handkerchiefs in Russia, so while I was wiping my face dry with the sleeve of my coat, I thought that maybe I still had a chance to live a good life after all.

We picked up our spoons and started eating. By his love God had saved me dozens of times to get me to this point. I wished that all my friends that did not make it could sit beside me to share the hope that I had at that moment.

Bedded down in a good, clean bed in that American camp, I wondered if I could improve my health so that I could walk through the villages of my ancestors once again. Or walk the fields and forest roads that I loved so much. Would I have enough food every day? Would I find my Mama, father and sisters in good health? Was there still a bed for me at home?

Without money, and out of touch with everything, it was clear that I needed God as much now as in Siberia. Could I still even write my name? When will I be able to put my arms around my mother? Will I be able to survive the stress of that moment? Or, will I drop to the floor and die from my pain? Will they all recognize me at home? Will they have a pair of socks set aside for me? Is my grandfather still alive? How can I greet him without dissolving in tears? Will it ever be possible to live this life in peace? Finally, I fell asleep.

Chapter 18
Canada

November, 1948

After a good night's rest, and a good breakfast, we left the American camp. We were now on our own and could travel to our destination by train.

There was no food for us on the way home. Oh, there was food and clothing everywhere, but I was without money. It was not that the after-war Germany was poor. The streets were filled with cars. The restaurants were full. And pedestrians were well dressed. It's just that Germany was not the land of caring, big hearted people.

The war had ended in May 1945, and now, it was November, 1948. Most of the destroyed towns and villages had been rebuilt.

I hoped to find a place at the railway station where I could report back. A place that could arrange transportation to a hospital. I needed a medical examination and special food because my digestive system could not function well enough to digest ordinary food. I also hoped to be able to see somebody like a psychiatrist. Perhaps there was a place where I could talk about my frustrations with a human society which sends their young men to be butchered in wars, and allows that the survivors can be systematically starved in slave labour camps. Maybe I could unload my pain in a two hour tear filled session, and then walk out a new man with a new beginning.

But there was nothing for us. Maybe it could have helped if somebody had just said, "Welcome home young man." But I never heard that. The indifference of my own nation was like a hand around my throat, trying to suffocate me.

While I walked down the street toward the railway station the rags hung out of my torn shoes and dragged on the sidewalk. I knew that the people for whom I had fought and suffered were indifferent to me, but I also knew that God did not desert me. He was with me in the trenches and in Siberia. He was also beside me now, while I walked down that street with a heavy heart.

At the station I boarded a train that brought me first to Frankfurt. There I was lucky. I had a plate full of soup from the Red Cross. I continued on a train to Saarbruken, right on the border of France.

Because it was a daylight ride, I saw dozens of beautiful villages and little towns on the way. I saw forests and fields as peaceful as could be, although it was a gray November day.

Would the sun ever shine again for me? Maybe. Maybe not. But the light of God was shining for me, much brighter than the sun, and because of that light I had peace in my heart despite all the hardship.

Near Bad Kreuznach we entered the French zone. A military guard got on the train. He looked at me and told me to step outside. He brought me to a small farm and locked me in an empty pig barn. After six hours he came back and told me to continue to Saarbruken, which was home to me. The French officer who locked me up with no explanation as to why, was no better than the Russians. He had nothing but cruelty for me. No food and no heart.

I arrived in Saarbruken at midnight. When I walked out of the station into a well illuminated square I again felt out of place. There were still hundreds of people strolling around, all wearing good clothe, and well nourished. And then, there was me. In rags. I certainly got a lot of attention.

One woman asked me where I came from. Another answered her, saying, "From Russia, can't you see that?" Some asked me if I had met their brothers or husbands. I knew how many had come to their end there, but I could not elaborate.

A young couple approached me. The woman asked me where I was going from here. When I told them that I had to go to Riegelsberg, her husband opened his briefcase and gave me money for the train.

By time it was one A.M. and I'd had nothing to eat since the soup in Frankfurt.

I left the circle of people and walked toward a Red Cross barracks. I knocked on the door and walked in. A friendly nurse looked up at me. After greeting her I asked politely if she had something for me to eat. She invited me to sit down. "Certainly I have something for you to eat," she said kindly. She then served me her own crumb cake and coffee. When I was finished I thanked that friendly soul and walked down the street to the tram stop. I arrived in Riegelsberg at 2:30 A.M..

I was lucky to find a young man in the street, and when I told him I was looking for my parents' house, he even walked there with me. He wished me all the best and left.

I rang the bell with my heart pounding. After awhile the door was opened and in the dark I could see a white-haired woman. All I could say was "Mama." When I went to embrace her she said, "I am not your mother, your mother lives upstairs." Then somebody turned on the light in the stairway and my mother called out, "Is that you, Herbert?" I said, "Yes, Mama, it's me!"

I walked up the stairs as fast as my ravished body could carry me. I embraced my dear mother and held on for a long time, wondering if I would now dissolve in tears and die. My two sisters, Martha and Gertrude, stood right and left of me. Then I turned around to embrace my father. I felt joy and immense pain at the same time.

Yes, there was a bed there for me!

My mother took my rags from me and disposed of them quickly. Then she brought me clean clothes. We talked until four in the morning, then we rushed to our beds to get a few hours of sleep.

In the morning my father had to leave to get to his office in the town of Saarbruken. I had all the time in the world to relax and enjoy a lengthy breakfast with my mother. So much had happened since we parted. The war was over, and all were alive in our family.

I soon discovered that it was not so easy to get away from the past. There was too much to forget: The Front

Line; the starvation and inhuman treatment in the slave camps in Russia. Those experiences kept intruding in my thoughts.

For three months all I did was walk the forest roads of the Saar country. I had breakfast early in the morning, left the house at dawn, and walked all day. I only came back at dusk, returning home to eat and sleep.

Most of the time my wanderings led me to a valley with a bubbling brook. Neither rain nor snow could keep me at home.

What I found in my wanderings was peace, freedom and beauty. I never carried food with me. I also never felt alone, because God, who loved me and shielded me from bullets, bombs and shells, was with me. He had pulled me up from my deathbed to go on living another day. Yes, I was alone, but I walked in his light, with joy, even on these dark wintery days.

One day I remembered a battle where I had absolutely no chance of survival. I stopped and asked myself why I had survived against all odds. For a moment I wondered if perhaps only my spirit was allowed to come home. I asked God to tell me if it was really I who walked in the forest. God said, "Step with your right foot into the mud. If you see your footprint, it is really you." I stepped forward into the mud and saw my footprint.

Still, I was not satisfied and asked Him how I had escaped death where almost everybody around me had died, and God said, "Have you forgotten me?"

At that moment I raised my arms staring up at the evening clouds. My tears ran freely and, despite the failing light of dusk, I envisioned the love, loyalty and power of God, and realized that I had never been alone.

While I walked through the valley of death God revealed himself to such an extent, and in such a dramatic way. If I had not come so often to my end and been pulled from the brink at the last moment, I would still be a doubter. God showed me his love and power. He also showed me my helplessness.

The fact that we were there together tied me to Jesus even more. I was a weak man who had come many times to the end. At each of those moments, he offered me his hand. Now we could walk together through this dark November evening. My sufferings were no longer a reason to complain, but an asset more precious than gold.

Forty years later I read Matthew 10-32, "And whoever does not accept his torture stake and follow after me, is not worthy of my name."

As I looked at the German situation all the high ideals preached over a thousand years vanished. Materialism was here to stay! Everybody for himself!

I still had many health problems, but I found an opportunity to learn the trade of cabinet-making. After two years I passed the course and was able to produce fine living room furniture.

While on vacation in Tyrol, I met Hildegard, a young woman from the Saar country. We were in love and decided to get married and go on to Canada. The problem, of course was how to manage it financially. I could not talk to my father about it. I turned to God. I stated my case, about the 2,000 DM it would take to finance it. Two

months later I had a bit of good fortune that provided me
with the 2,000 DM I needed.

July, 1956

Our wedding took place in a small chapel near the Blies
River. Hildegard was only twenty years old at that time.

A few months later we packed our belongings and said
good bye to parents, sisters and brothers. We also said fare-
well to our motherland. It was not easy for either of us.

We took passage on the M.S. Seven Seas, boarding at
Brest, France.

Our ship plowed westward through green waters. The
air was gratifyingly pure and salty. We enjoyed the time
at sea. It was an experience we had never had before. We
looked forward to a new life, where nobody talked about
war and the tears and sufferings that go with it.

Nine days later we arrived at Montreal, Quebec.

Our new life in Canada would have been much more
difficult if it had not been for the Gascon family, Rosaire
and Blanche Yvonne and their four children. They made us
feel so much at home with all the love they poured out to
us.

2003

The last forty-seven years have rushed by. While I was
busy carving out a life for my family, I sometimes forgot
to pray, but not for long. I always returned to prayer and
thanksgiving. My faith was indestructible.

Several years ago, my friend Horst, who built a cottage
not far from me, had to cut several trees. I knew that he

had difficulties with his neck, so when I heard his chainsaw going I went over to give him a hand. I did the cutting and he stood about six meters behind me to watch,

I was cutting the last tree around noon when I felt that Horst stood directly behind me. I wondered why he would do that, since I could not move either to left or right because my way was blocked by branches. Now I would also not be able to run backwards if I had to.

My saw bit deeper and deeper into the maple tree. When it broke, I was pulled sharply to the right. A branch 25 centimeters in diameter, and about 13 meters long fell from a 13 meter height.

The branch would have struck my head, but because Horst pulled me to the right, it only touched my left hand and hit the ground with a thud, just beside my left foot.

Horst was white and near tears when I asked him how it happened that he was directly behind me. He was equally puzzled. He said, "Yes, why was I behind you?" Horst had saved my life, but was he not a tool of God?

I am now 79 years of age and in excellent health. I thank God every morning for giving me so much strength. I plant a garden in the summer and do some woodcutting in the fall and winter. I need strength to pull my toboggan, loaded with food and materials, along a three kilometer stretch of a bush road, sometimes through deep snow, to get to my cottage.

I have not asked for miracles, but I have often asked why God did so much for me. One day, reading Psalm 91, I found many parallels to my own life.

What have I learned in all these years? I have learned to

trust, and to love God. I know that Jesus keeps his promises. Before He went back to His father, He promised that
He would be with us to the end of time. With whom will
He be? With the ones who love Him and talk to Him, of
course. He has kept His word, when He said: "I am going
now, to prepare a place for you." With all His love and
power, He will certainly do so.

I stand in awe before God, who was, is and will be
forever, my savior and my only light.

*****